The Balanced Relationship Blueprint

Ancient Techniques for Modern Love

and Conscious Parenting

Table of Contents

Authors Bio
Chapter 1: Connecting the Past to the Present
Chapter 2: The Foundations of Love
Chapter 3 Embracing the Divine Feminine
Chapter 4 Honouring the Divine Masculine
Chapter 5: The Dance of Energies
Chapter 6: The Art of Communication
Chapter 7: Achieving Harmony through Conflict Resolution
Chapter 8: Sensuality and Intimacy
Chapter 9: Raising Children with Ancient Wisdom
Chapter 10: Nurturing Masculine and Feminine Energies in Children
Chapter 11: Rituals and Practices for Modern Couples
Chapter 12: Enduring Love

Authors Bio

With nearly two decades of experience as a Relationship and Family Coach, Nichole Farrow is a leading expert in her field. Her coaching practice spans various settings, from the corporate world to the intricacies of personal relationships and blended families. Certified in Neuro-Linguistic Programming and human needs psychology, Nichole brings a multi-faceted approach to her work, blending scientific methodologies with intuitive insights.
Nichole's venture into this field is deeply personal. As a child of divorce and a member of a blended family, she has firsthand experience navigating the emotional complexities that come with familial transitions. Her own journey through divorce and into a fulfilling second marriage has further enriched her understanding, making her a compassionate and relatable guide for those facing similar life changes.

Beyond theoretical knowledge, Nichole offers practical strategies rooted in real-world experience. Her profound understanding of human behaviour and relationship dynamics enables her to provide actionable insights. She specialises in bridging time-tested wisdom with the realities of contemporary love, family life, and the unique challenges posed by the digital age.

Nichole's brand ethos—to educate, motivate, and inspire—resonates throughout her work, whether it's in one-on-one coaching sessions, digital courses, retreats, or memberships. She has developed a comprehensive range of services that not only address immediate relationship concerns but also equip individuals and couples with the tools for long-term happiness and success.

As a thought leader in her field, Nichole frequently contributes articles, appears on podcasts, and speaks at events. Her insights have guided numerous individuals and couples through the complexities of love and intimacy, empowering them to build enduring and enriching relationships.

Outside of her coaching practice, Nichole is committed to her own personal growth and transformation. She embodies the principles she teaches, constantly striving to elevate her own relationships and those of her clients. This dedication to both personal and professional development establishes Nichole Farrow as an expert in the realm of modern relationships and family dynamics.

Chapter 1: Connecting the Past to the Present

In today's fast-paced world, filled with notifications, busy schedules, and competing priorities, it's easy for couples to drift apart. The modern world has brought countless advantages, but it has also presented unique challenges for relationships. The vibrancy of initial love often fades into the background, replaced by the humdrum of daily tasks and digital distractions. Add children and external pressures such as work, and social expectations into the mix and it is no wonder many couples find themselves unfulfilled, and in some cases leaving their relationships in search of a deeper connection. As a relationship and family coach, and before that a corporate performance coach, I have had unprecedented insight into human connections, emotions, needs and desires. Having worked with many couples trying to save their marriage as well as those who have decided to divorce or remarry, I have come to realise we all want the same thing, to love, be loved and be happy. To quote the great Tony Robbins the quality of our relationships determines the quality of our lives and we are all searching for that extraordinary love that elevates us, to be with someone we can create and share a beautiful life with. As emotionally intelligent tribal creatures our need for love and connection is primal. While our surroundings, lifestyles, and challenges have evolved, the human heart's essential needs - to be loved, understood, and cherished - have remained constant.

Today we have the benefit of technology that can connect us instantly with people all over the world and yet we are more stressed, lonely and self-critical than ever. Too preoccupied with trying to keep up with everyone else and making unhealthy comparisons with the perfect lives we see on social media, to take care of our own. This can leave us feeling deficient and constantly chasing something unattainable. In my experience most couples face the same challenges and problems: lack of communication, intimacy, and time. Coupled with the growing social pressure to be all and have it all, these issues left unchecked can create a chasm in relationships, and ultimately lead to unhappiness, toxic behaviour and divorce. And the problem doesn't stop there. This behaviour is setting an unhealthy perception of love for the next generation, we are all products of our environment, our conditioning in childhood programmes our subconscious that runs our adult lives. So if we can't create deep meaningful happy relationships today we are condemning our children to more of the same in the future. As a child of divorce and a divorcee myself I understand first-hand the pain and lasting damage toxic relationships can have on a family and the next generation. It is my own personal journey of self-discovery and need for understanding that led me to delve into human needs psychology, relationship dynamics and behaviour. Understanding the problem was one thing, solving it is another. How do we create a loving fulfilling relationship today? The kind of soulful understanding that seems almost mythical in its depth and completely unachievable in today's flippant world.

If technology is part of the problem, and human emotions at their core have remained unchanged, then I needed to go back to a time when the connection was deeper and there were fewer distractions to find the answers.

Enter the ancient world of our ancestors. Civilisations that existed long before us - the Egyptians with their divine concepts of partnership, the Greeks with their philosophical ideals of love, and the Indian subcontinent with its ancient treatises on relationships - had profound insights into love, connection, and balance. Each of these cultures, in their own ways, had found paths to the deep, enduring love that many of us seek today.

I wrote this book to enhance modern relationships by blending the timeless teachings of the past with our contemporary understanding. It is my aim for this book to inspire a fresh vision for your relationships, one that seamlessly melds timeless teachings with today's unique challenges. To rejuvenate and deepen your current bonds but also equip you with the knowledge and strategies to nurture lasting relationships that stand as a legacy of love, understanding, and purpose that will inspire and shape future generations.

If you're looking to create an extraordinary relationship that thrives in the modern world this book offers you a deep dive into relationship principles that remain as potent today as they were years ago, bringing both depth and authenticity to modern love and relationships. Together we'll delve deep into rituals, philosophies, and practices that were once integral to ancient societies and explore how they can be integrated into today's fast-paced life.

We'll rediscover the enchanting dance of masculine and feminine energies, a balance that, when struck correctly, can elevate a relationship to unparalleled heights. We'll explore timeless rituals, these big and small rituals are designed to deepen the bond, reignite the passion, and create and nurture an enduring connection.

Furthermore, beyond rituals and practices, this book will empower you with the age-old secrets of sustaining love. We'll discover tools, perspectives, and practices that will infuse your relationship with depth, passion, and a sense of sacredness.

In an age where everything is transient and fleeting, where relationships often buckle under external pressures, I invite you to discover a love that's enduring, profound, and deeply enriching. It's an invitation to journey together, hand in hand, drawing from the past's reservoir of wisdom to craft a happy fulfilling relationship today.

Chapter 2: The Foundations of Love

The ancient Egyptians, with their grand pyramids and intricate hieroglyphs, viewed love as the very essence of creation. They built temples and monuments dedicated to gods and goddesses of love and fertility, standing as majestic testaments to the reverence they held for this divine emotion. But the Egyptians were not alone in this quest to understand love. From the Greeks to the Chinese, from Native American tribes to African cultures, the pursuit of love and the understanding of its complexities have been a universal endeavour.

Fast forward to today, and our temples of love have evolved into our homes and the intimate spaces we create with our partners. While we no longer erect grand physical structures to commemorate love, the monuments we build within our hearts and minds are just as significant. These emotional and psychological structures are shaped by shared experiences, deepened by mutual trust, and fortified with the understanding and appreciation of each other's individuality.

While times have changed and societies have evolved, the core tenets of love have remained timeless and universal. These core foundations are just as fundamental today for building fulfilling and lasting relationships as they were in ancient times.

We all know that strong foundations are critical to building anything long-lasting, and our relationships are no different. In order to create a deep, fulfilling and resilient relationship we have to have a strong foundation. Only then can you create an exceptional life together, because your relationship forms the foundation on which everything else in your life is built. In this chapter, we will delve into the core principles of such a foundation and how to create it today.

Mutual Respect
In the ancient world, mutual respect was considered the bedrock of a successful partnership. The Egyptians, with their intricate hieroglyphs, and the Greeks, with their concept of 'Pragma,' both emphasised the importance of a balanced, respectful relationship. Fast forward to today, and the essence of mutual respect remains unchanged and more important than ever as the dynamics of modern relationships have evolved to include new complexities such as shifting gender roles, work-life balance, and shared responsibilities within the household.

Mutual respect is not just a lofty ideal; it's a practical, actionable principle that serves as the foundation for all other aspects of a relationship. It's the soil in which love, trust, and emotional intimacy grow. Without it, even the most passionate love can erode over time, leaving behind a relationship that's devoid of substance and meaning.

In the context of today's fast-paced life, mutual respect manifests in various ways. It's seen in the equitable division of household chores, acknowledging that both partners contribute to maintaining a home. It's reflected in the support you offer each other as you juggle professional responsibilities, understanding that both careers are equally important. And it's evident in how you navigate the challenges of parenting, recognising that both of you bring unique strengths to the table.

One of the most powerful ways to cultivate mutual respect is through active listening. This involves not just hearing what your partner is saying, but truly understanding their perspective, validating their feelings, and responding thoughtfully. Active listening creates a sense of equality and honours your partner's individuality, creating a safe space for open dialogue and emotional vulnerability.

Moreover, mutual respect extends to recognising and appreciating each other's contributions, both big and small. Whether it's a grand gesture like planning a surprise getaway or something as simple as taking out the rubbish without being asked, these acts are acknowledgements of each other's efforts and roles within the relationship. They serve as daily affirmations that say, "I see you, I appreciate you, and I value what you bring to our partnership."

In a world where individual achievements are often celebrated more than collective efforts, it's crucial to remember that a relationship is a team endeavour. When both partners feel valued and respected, they are more likely to invest in shared goals, whether it's buying a home, raising compassionate children, or simply creating a life filled with joy and purpose.

By making mutual respect a core value in your relationship, you're not just creating a healthy dynamic between two individuals; you're also setting the stage for a partnership that can withstand the tests of time and circumstance. It becomes a living example of what a balanced, fulfilling relationship should look like, serving as a legacy for future generations to emulate.

So, as you navigate the complexities of modern love, remember that mutual respect is the eternal bedrock upon which all enduring relationships are built. Make it a daily practice, a non-negotiable standard, and watch how it transforms not just your relationship, but also the quality of your life.

Shared Values

In ancient civilisations, shared values were celebrated and reinforced through rituals and ceremonies. The Egyptians, for instance, had annual festivals dedicated to goddesses like Hathor, where couples would renew their commitments based on shared beliefs. Similarly, in Hindu culture, the Saptapadi ritual involves couples taking seven steps around a sacred fire, each step symbolising a different marital vow that reflects shared values.

In the context of modern relationships, shared values serve as the invisible thread that binds you and your partner together. They are the foundational pillars that not only support but also direct the trajectory of your relationship. These values act as a blueprint for how to experience and view the world and help you navigate the complexities and challenges of contemporary life. Whether it's your approach to finances, your views on parenting, or your commitment to personal growth, having shared values provides a sense of unity and direction.

Nowadays a lot of people meet through dating apps. These platforms have revolutionised modern dating, but they often focus on matching individuals based on interests rather than values and this is where it can often go wrong. While it's great to find someone who also enjoys travelling or appreciates fine wine, these common interests are not the elements that will sustain a relationship in the long run. Imagine one partner values fun and excitement above all else, while the other prioritises family and stability. No amount of shared hobbies or interests will bridge that fundamental gap. Over time, these differing values will create friction, leading to misunderstandings, and ultimately, driving the couple apart.

In contrast, when you share core values, you have a much stronger foundation to build upon. You're more likely to make decisions that benefit both of you, and you'll find it easier to compromise because you're both working towards the same ultimate goals. Shared values are the compass that keeps you moving in the same direction, even when you encounter obstacles or need to take detours.

One of the most enlightening exercises a couple can undertake is to sit down and discuss their individual and shared values. This isn't just a one-time conversation but should be an ongoing dialogue that evolves as you both grow and change. Understanding what you both hold dear can help you make decisions that honour those values, whether it's choosing a place to live, planning a family, or even deciding how to spend your free time.

So, as you navigate the labyrinth of modern love, remember that shared values are your guiding light. They are what will make or break your relationship, not the superficial interests that may have initially drawn you together. Make it a priority to identify, discuss, and honour these values, and you'll find that they become the glue that holds your relationship together, ensuring that it not only survives but thrives in today's complex world.

Effective Communication

In ancient Egyptian lore, tales abound of lovers overcoming insurmountable odds through the power of dialogue and mutual understanding. Similarly, Native American tribes held storytelling in high regard, using it as a medium to pass down wisdom about love, relationships, and the complexities of human interaction.

Fast forward to today, and the essence of those ancient practices remains relevant: effective communication is the lifeblood of any enduring relationship. In my line of work, I've found that the most common issue plaguing couples is a breakdown in communication. This isn't just a minor hiccup; it's often the catalyst for emotional pain, misunderstandings, and, in many cases, divorce. But what does effective communication really entail? This is so key there is a whole chapter on it later in the book, but for now, let me say as a core principle it's far more than just talking or sharing information. It's about creating a sanctuary—a safe space where both partners can openly express their needs, desires, and concerns without fear of judgement. It's about active listening, where you're not just hearing the words but also understanding the emotions and intentions behind them.

One of the most significant problems I encounter with couples is the assumption that their partner is a mind reader—that love alone is enough to make each person intuitively aware of the other's needs. This is a dangerous misconception. No one is a mind reader, and many of life's misunderstandings and disappointments stem from this false expectation.

Having a meta-conversation about how you both prefer to communicate can be a game-changer. Do you need time to process information before discussing it? Do you prefer directness, or do you appreciate a more nuanced approach? Understanding each other's communication styles can prevent a lot of unnecessary heartache. It helps to close the gaps where things have been left unsaid, or worse, where assumptions have been made that lead to conflict or emotional distance. Bringing consciousness into your communication practices can significantly strengthen your relationship. It equips you both with the tools to navigate misunderstandings and to weather relational storms. When you communicate effectively, you're not just solving immediate issues; you're also building a reservoir of emotional intelligence and mutual respect.

This reservoir becomes your go-to resource in times of conflict, enabling you to resolve issues more efficiently and with greater empathy.

So, as you journey through the landscape of love and commitment, remember that effective communication is your lifeline. It's the tool that allows you to dig deep, to unearth the roots of issues rather than merely trimming their outward manifestations. By investing in open, honest, and conscious communication, you're not just avoiding pitfalls; you're paving the road for a relationship that's both resilient and deeply fulfilling.

Rituals of Connection

From the grandeur of elaborate Egyptian marriage ceremonies to the simplicity of daily offerings to deities representing love, rituals have been an integral part of human relationships for millennia. The Chinese philosophy of Yin and Yang also underscores the importance of balance and harmony, often maintained through daily rituals and practices that bring equilibrium to relationships.

This book is filled with rituals—both ancient and modern—that are designed to elevate your relationship and family life. These rituals serve as a bridge, connecting the tried and tested wisdom of the past with the unique challenges and opportunities of contemporary love.

Today, rituals can take various forms, from a daily emotional check-in to weekly date nights or even annual getaways. These aren't just activities; they're shared practices that create moments of reconnection, helping you navigate the inevitable ups and downs of life. They serve as touchstones, grounding your relationship in a shared history while simultaneously creating new memories that enrich your partnership.

How often do you check in with each other about your emotional well-being? And I don't mean just talking about the kids, work, or social commitments. How often do you focus solely on each other's emotional needs and the health of your relationship? Creating a dedicated time and space to do this on a regular basis—by which I mean at least weekly—can work wonders for your relationship. These rituals become the pillars that uphold your relationship, offering a structured way to infuse your partnership with meaning, intention, and connection. They turn ordinary moments into sacred experiences, elevating the mundane into the extraordinary. Whether it's a simple act like leaving love notes for each other or something more elaborate like an annual ritual where you renew your vows, these practices become the heartbeat of your relationship.

In a world where distractions are abundant and time seems scarce, rituals offer a way to slow down, focus on what's truly important, and consciously celebrate the love that you share. They become the lens through which you see each other anew, each and every day, fortifying your bond and deepening your connection with each passing year.

So, as you navigate the complexities of modern love, I invite you to explore the rituals outlined in this book. They are your gateway to a more fulfilling, more enriching, and more resilient relationship—one that not only stands the test of time but also serves as a beacon of what love can be.

Touch The Language of the Soul

In the annals of history, the power of touch has been celebrated as a vital component of human connection. The Greek concept of 'Eros,' the son of Aphrodite, personified intense love and desire and emphasised the importance of physical love and attraction. Similarly, Ancient Egyptian art often depicts couples in various forms of touch—be it a hand on the shoulder or fingers entwined.

Fast forward to today's digital age, and we find ourselves in a paradox. While technology has made it easier to connect with people worldwide, it has also created a physical disconnect between couples. It's not uncommon to see partners sitting next to each other in bed or at opposite ends of the sofa, engrossed in their phones rather than in each other. This lack of physical intimacy is often cited as a leading cause of infidelity and divorce. But intimacy doesn't just mean sex; it encompasses a broader range of physical interactions that serve as daily affirmations of love. The power of a simple hug, a kiss, or even a fleeting touch cannot be overstated—especially if your partner's primary love language is physical touch. We'll delve deeper into love languages and the nuances of intimacy in later chapters, but it's crucial to understand that touch acts as another key pillar of love. These gestures are not just acts; they are affirmations that love is not solely an emotional or intellectual experience but a physical one, felt in every fibre of our being.

Touch serves as a language of the soul, a form of communication that words often fail to capture. It's a way to say, "I'm here, I love you, and you're important to me," without uttering a single word. It's a way to bridge emotional distances and to reaffirm your presence in each other's lives. It's a way to bring the focus back to the 'here and now,' pulling you both away from the myriad distractions that modern life throws your way.

So, as you navigate the complexities of love in a world filled with digital distractions, remember the irreplaceable power of touch. Make it a point to integrate these simple yet profound gestures into your daily life. Whether it's holding hands while watching a movie, giving each other a hug before heading out the door, or simply placing a hand on your partner's shoulder as you pass by, these acts of touch become the building blocks of a deeper, more intimate connection. The power of touch serves as a grounding force, a reminder of the tangible, physical love that forms the bedrock of any enduring relationship.

Growth and Evolution

Ancient civilisations from various corners of the world understood the dynamic nature of love and relationships. For instance, the Greeks had a nuanced understanding of love, breaking it down into different types—Agape, Eros, Philia, and Storge—each representing a different stage or form of love. In Hindu philosophy, the concept of 'Dharma' emphasises the importance of duty, virtue, and moral life, which includes the mutual growth and responsibilities of a marital relationship. These ancient cultures were keenly aware that love was not a static experience but a fluid journey that required continual nurturing and adaptation.

In today's rapidly changing world, this ancient wisdom holds more relevance than ever. With longer life expectancies and an ever-expanding array of opportunities for personal and professional growth, the commitment of "till death do us part" has become a marathon, not a sprint. Over such a long journey, change is not just inevitable; it's a given.
Understanding the nuances between growing apart and growing together is crucial in this context. Growing apart doesn't necessarily signify a failure in the relationship; it may simply mean that the paths you both are on have diverged. This is a natural part of human evolution and can be an important, albeit difficult, phase of personal growth.

Conversely, growing together means that both partners are evolving in ways that make the relationship stronger, richer, and more fulfilling. It's about synergistic growth, where the sum is greater than its parts. When you grow together, you're not just enduring life's challenges; you're leveraging them to reach new heights—heights that might have been unattainable or would have taken much longer to reach on your own.

This kind of mutual growth requires adaptability and a willingness to learn from each other and the relationship itself. It could mean supporting each other's career changes, embarking on spiritual journeys together, or even exploring new cultures and philosophies that enrich your understanding of love and commitment. The key is to be open to change and to view it not as a threat but as an opportunity for mutual growth and deeper connection.

In a world where the only constant is change, your ability to adapt and grow together is the foundation of a lasting, fulfilling relationship. So, as you navigate the complexities of modern love, remember to draw from the well of ancient wisdom—from the Greeks' multifaceted understanding of love to the Hindu concept of 'Dharma.' These age-old philosophies remind us that love's true nature is dynamic, requiring both partners to be active participants in its ongoing evolution.

Trust

In relationships, trust stands as a pivotal pillar. In Jewish culture, the concept of 'Shalom Bayit'—peace in the home—emphasises the importance of a harmonious domestic environment, one that is fundamentally built on trust. In Hindu mythology, the epic tale of Rama and Sita serves as a timeless narrative of trust, loyalty, and the trials that can test a relationship.

Trust is not merely an emotional luxury; it's a necessity. It's the unspoken assurance that your partner will stand by you through thick and thin, in joy and sorrow, triumph and defeat. Building and maintaining this trust demands consistent effort, open communication, honesty, and a steadfast commitment to each other. It's the foundation upon which all other relationship dynamics are built, from mutual respect to effective communication.

In my line of work, I often encounter the question: Can a relationship survive, let alone thrive, after trust has been broken? This question becomes particularly poignant in cases involving infidelity. The answer is yes, but it's neither simple nor quick. It requires a monumental amount of work, time, forgiveness, and compassion from both parties involved. Trust is the most crucial value you can have in a relationship; without it, reaching the extraordinary heights of a deep, meaningful connection is virtually impossible.

When trust is the bedrock of your relationship, it becomes a powerful platform for building the life you envision for yourself and your family. It's not just about the love between two individuals but also about creating an environment where everyone thrives. In such a setting, children learn the values of mutual respect, effective communication, and unconditional love, thereby setting the stage for a lasting legacy that impacts generations to come.

The wisdom of ancient civilisations serves as a lighthouse in this endeavour. For instance, in traditional Japanese culture, there's a practice known as Kintsugi, where broken pottery is repaired with gold, acknowledging the fractures rather than hiding them. The result is an object that's more beautiful for having been broken and repaired. This serves as a metaphor for relationships as well—when trust is broken and then painstakingly rebuilt, the relationship can emerge stronger, more aware of its vulnerabilities, and more committed to ongoing growth and integrity.

Chapter 3 Embracing the Divine Feminine

In a world that often prioritises masculine energy—defined by logic, competition, and outward achievement—it's easy to overlook the vital role the Divine Feminine plays in our lives, especially in the realm of romantic relationships. The Divine Feminine, characterised by intuition, emotional depth, nurturing, and receptivity, is not confined to any gender. It is an essential aspect of the human psyche that exists in everyone, irrespective of their biological sex. Similarly, the Divine Masculine, with its attributes of action, logic, and strength, is also a universal energy that each of us carries within.

The importance of embracing both these energies becomes particularly evident in romantic relationships. In a partnership, the balance of the Divine Feminine and Masculine energies contributes to a more harmonious, respectful, and deeply connected union. When we lean too heavily into one energy, whether it be masculine or feminine, we risk creating an imbalance that can manifest as emotional distance, misunderstanding, or even conflict. For example, a relationship dominated by masculine energy may lack emotional depth and nurturing, becoming a mere transactional interaction that lacks soulful connection. On the other hand, a relationship overly steeped in feminine energy may lack boundaries and direction, leading to co-dependency or stagnation. The key to a fulfilling, loving relationship lies in the integration and balance of these divine energies within each partner and the relationship as a whole.

In a society that often equates strength with masculinity and vulnerability with femininity, acknowledging and embracing the Divine Feminine becomes an act of courage. It allows men to explore their emotional depth, to become more receptive, and to engage in a more nurturing form of strength. For women, it offers a way to reclaim the power and wisdom that society has often dismissed or suppressed. And for those who identify outside the gender binary, the Divine Feminine and Masculine offer a framework for balance and wholeness that transcends societal norms.

This chapter aims to delve into the profound impact the Divine Feminine can have on romantic relationships. We will explore how both men and women can cultivate this energy to nurture greater love, understanding, and connection with their partners. We will also discuss the importance of balancing this with the Divine Masculine, especially in a world that often tips the scales in favour of masculine attributes. Through real-world examples, ancient wisdom, and practical advice, this chapter will serve as a guide of how to enrich your romantic relationship through the harmonious integration of both the Divine Feminine and Masculine energies.

In the vast expanse of human history, civilisations from every corner of the Earth have revered the concept of the Divine Feminine. Whether she is depicted as Gaia, the primordial Earth Goddess of ancient Greece, or as the compassionate Kuan Yin in Eastern traditions, the Divine Feminine has always been a symbol of creation, nurture, wisdom, and strength. As society evolved, the essence of this divine energy was overshadowed by patriarchal systems and values. However, today there is a palpable resurgence of interest and reverence for the Divine Feminine, as people everywhere begin to recognise and celebrate her power and grace.

Her Power

The power of the Divine Feminine is multifaceted. She is both the fierce warrior and the gentle caregiver. Her strength is evident in the protective love of a mother, the resilience of women throughout history, and the passionate fury of a goddess scorned.

Creation: The Cosmic Womb

One of the most profound aspects of the Divine Feminine is her role in creation. In almost every culture, legends speak of goddesses who birthed the universe, the stars, and all of life. This creative energy isn't just about physical birth but extends to the birth of ideas, art, and transformation. In Hindu mythology, for instance, the goddess Saraswati is the embodiment of wisdom, music, and the arts. She represents the creative and transformative power of the Divine Feminine. In ancient times women were worshipped as life-givers, in the Divine Feminine image. Today there is growing pressure on mothers to get back into their jeans and go back to work after having a baby. Driven by the need to keep up with unrealistic expectations set by the media and celebrity culture, and the lack of support to parents caused by families living more dispersed these days, many mothers feel isolated, exhausted and ashamed of their postnatal bodies and struggling. Rather than embracing the beautiful, powerful Divine Feminine being that they are. We as a society need to do better but within your relationship, you can also choose to worship the creative mother and her body. Beyond physical birth, giving yourselves permission to unleash your creativity as individuals and together will create flow and excitement as you build the life of your dreams together.

Intuition: The Inner Oracle
Intuition, often considered the "Inner Oracle," is a vital aspect of the Divine Feminine. This isn't merely about psychic abilities or mystical experiences; it's about a

deep-seated wisdom that resides within each of us. This inherent knowing guides us through life's complexities, offering insights that logic and reason may not provide. In Celtic traditions, the goddess Brigid was revered as a deity of inspiration and prophecy, embodying this intuitive aspect of the Divine Feminine. By bringing consciousness to our intuition and the forces around us, we can align with their wisdom and tap into their guidance.

For example, the moon, with its ever-changing phases, serves as a powerful symbol and tool for intuitive work. Each phase of the moon offers a unique energy that can be harnessed for different aspects of life.

- **New Moon:** A time for setting new intentions and planting seeds for future endeavours. This is an excellent time for meditative practices that focus on new beginnings and aspirations.

- **Waxing Moon:** As the moon grows, so should your focus and efforts toward the intentions set during the new moon. This is a time for action and forward momentum.

- **Full Moon:** A period of fruition and reflection. The full moon illuminates both the external world and our inner landscape, making it a potent time for intuitive insights.

- **Waning Moon:** As the moon diminishes in size, it's a period for release and letting go. This is a time to shed old habits, thoughts, or relationships that no longer serve you.

By aligning your activities and meditative practices with these moon phases, you can tap into the cyclical wisdom of the Divine Feminine and bolster your intuitive capabilities.

Meditation itself serves as a direct channel to access your intuition. Here are some meditation practices specifically designed to enhance your intuitive faculties:

- **Third Eye Meditation:** Focus on the area between your eyebrows, often considered the seat of intuition in various spiritual traditions. Visualise it as a radiant indigo light, pulsating with wisdom and insight.

- **Guided Imagery:** Use a guided meditation that takes you on a journey to meet your "inner sage" or intuitive self. Listen to the wisdom this inner guide has to offer.

- **Body Scan:** Often our bodies hold intuitive wisdom that our minds overlook. A body scan meditation can help you tune into bodily sensations that may offer intuitive guidance.

Keeping a journal can be another transformative practice for enhancing intuition. Make it a habit to jot down your dreams, hunches, or gut feelings. Over time, you'll start to see patterns and gain insights that can guide you in making more aligned choices.

Many ancient cultures employed divination tools to access wisdom beyond the ordinary senses. Tarot cards, runes, or the I Ching can serve as powerful mediums to channel intuitive insights. While these tools have specific symbolic frameworks, your personal interpretation and intuition are crucial for gaining meaningful guidance.

Being fully present in the moment enhances your ability to tap into intuitive wisdom. Practices like mindful walking, eating, or simply breathing can serve as gateways to deeper intuitive understanding.

Intuition is not a gift bestowed upon a chosen few but a skill that can be cultivated and refined. By aligning with natural cycles like the moon phases, engaging in intuitive-enhancing meditative practices, and employing tools like journaling and divination, you can tap into the rich reservoir of wisdom that resides within you. In doing so, you align with the Divine Feminine's intuitive aspect, enriching your life with insights and guidance that reason alone could never offer.

Nurturing: The Earthly Mother

The Divine Feminine, often symbolised by the Earth or "Mother Earth," embodies the nurturing qualities that sustain and nourish all life. In Native American traditions, this nurturing entity is often referred to as "Pachamama." She provides for us, sustains us, and teaches us the virtues of care, understanding, and healing. Just as the Earth offers us sustenance and shelter, the Divine Feminine energy within us encourages us to nurture ourselves and others. This nurturing aspect is not just a metaphor but a practical guide for emotional well-being, especially in today's fast-paced, technology-driven world. Being in nature has been scientifically proven to improve mental health. It reduces stress hormones, lowers anxiety, improves mood, and increases feelings of happiness and well-being. Going for a walk or a hike, forest bathing or grounding yourself in nature. These practices have been shown to reduce inflammation, improve sleep, and increase well-being.

Her Grace

Grace, in the context of the Divine Feminine, is about moving through life with ease, with understanding, and with a deep sense of peace.

Receptivity: The Sacred Chalice

The concept of Receptivity, often associated with the Divine Feminine, is a powerful yet misunderstood aspect of balanced relationships. Unlike the Divine Masculine, which is often characterised by action, direction, and outward focus, the Divine Feminine embodies the art of receiving. This is not a passive state but a conscious choice to remain open, to absorb, and to allow things to flow inward. In Taoist philosophy, this is encapsulated in the concept of Yin, which serves as a counterbalance to the active Yang.

Being receptive means creating a space within yourself where you can receive love, wisdom, and even criticism, and use it for personal and relational growth. It's about listening as much as speaking, about understanding as much as being understood. This receptivity is not just emotional but also intellectual and spiritual. It allows you to absorb experiences, learn from them, and integrate them into your life and relationship.

In a practical sense, being receptive could mean listening deeply to your partner's concerns without immediately offering solutions, or it could mean being open to new experiences that your partner brings into the relationship. It's about being emotionally available to receive your partner's love, and also about being intellectually open to consider their point of view, even if it challenges your own beliefs or comfort zones.

This quality of receptivity also extends to how you interact with the world around you. It's about being open to new experiences, wisdom, and even challenges, and absorbing them in a way that enriches your life and relationship. It's a form of active engagement with life, a way of saying 'yes' to the universe and allowing it to nourish you in return.

So, in your journey towards a balanced relationship, don't underestimate the power of the Divine Feminine's receptivity. It's not a sign of weakness but a testament to the strength that comes from openness, from the ability to receive and grow. By embracing this quality, you not only enrich your own life but also bring a deeper, more meaningful form of engagement to your relationship.

Strength in Unity: The Web of Life
The principle of "Strength in Unity" is a key element of the Divine Feminine, emphasising the power that comes from collective action, mutual support, and interconnectedness. Unlike the individualistic or competitive tendencies often associated with the Divine Masculine, the Divine Feminine seeks to build bridges, forge connections, and create a web of life where each strand supports the other. This is beautifully encapsulated in African philosophies like "Ubuntu," which translates to "I am because we are." It's a concept that embodies the Divine Feminine

principle of collective strength and interdependence. This idea is not just philosophical but deeply rooted in our human experience. The need to find our tribe, to connect with a mate, and to belong to a community is primal. It's hardwired into our DNA because, from an evolutionary standpoint, there is safety and strength in numbers. But beyond mere survival, there is a profound emotional and spiritual fulfilment that comes from being part of something greater than oneself.

In the context of a relationship, "Strength in Unity" means recognising that while each partner is a complete individual, there is a unique power that arises when two people come together in a balanced, harmonious union. It's about moving from a 'me' to a 'we' mindset, where the focus shifts from individual accomplishments to shared goals and dreams. It's about understanding that each partner brings something valuable to the relationship, and these individual contributions become exponentially more powerful when united. This principle encourages couples to collaborate rather than compete, to support each other's individual dreams while also working towards shared goals. It's about creating a relationship where both partners feel seen, heard, and valued, and where the sum is indeed greater than its parts.

In a world that often promotes individual achievement at the expense of collective well-being, embracing the Divine Feminine principle of "Strength in Unity" serves as a powerful counter-narrative. It reminds us that our greatest achievements, both personally and relationally, come from our ability to work together, to support each other, and to recognise the interconnectedness of all life. By adopting this mindset, we not only enrich our own relationships but also contribute to a more harmonious, unified world.

Empathy: The Heart of Compassion
Empathy, often considered the heart of compassion, is a defining characteristic of the Divine Feminine. This quality allows her to connect deeply with others, to feel their joys and sorrows as if they were her own, and to offer unconditional love and understanding. In Buddhist traditions, this empathetic energy is personified in the goddess Tara, often depicted as a nurturing mother figure who offers solace and guidance to those in distress. She is a symbol of the Divine Feminine's ability to feel with others, not just for them, and to offer a sanctuary of emotional and spiritual support.

In the context of a relationship, empathy becomes a transformative force. It's the ability to put yourself in your partner's shoes, to understand their perspective without judgement, and to validate their feelings even if you don't necessarily agree with them. This kind of empathetic connection creates a safe space where both partners can be vulnerable, open, and authentic with each other. It creates a level of emotional intimacy that goes beyond mere companionship, delving into the realm of deep, soulful connection.

But empathy in a relationship isn't just about big, emotional moments; it's also about the small, everyday interactions. It's the gentle touch when your partner is stressed, the listening ear when they've had a hard day, and the encouraging word when they're facing a challenge. These small acts of empathy accumulate over time, creating a reservoir of goodwill and affection that can help sustain the relationship through more challenging periods.

Moreover, empathy has a ripple effect. When one partner practises empathy, it often encourages the other to do the same, creating a virtuous cycle of mutual understanding and respect. This is particularly important in times of conflict or misunderstanding, where empathy can serve as a bridge, helping to heal divides and restore harmony.

Empathy also extends beyond the relationship to the wider community and world. An empathetic individual is more likely to engage in acts of kindness and compassion, not just towards their partner but towards others as well. In this way, the Divine

Feminine's quality of empathy serves as a guiding light, encouraging us to be better partners, better community members, and ultimately, better human beings.

In a world that often seems driven by self-interest and division, the Divine Feminine's gift of empathy offers a different path. It invites us to connect, to feel, and to love deeply, reminding us that at the core of our human experience is the simple, yet profound, ability to understand and be understood. By embracing this empathetic energy, we not only enrich our own lives and relationships but also contribute to a more compassionate and harmonious world.

So how do you embrace these Divine Feminine traits in a world that often seems driven by aggression, haste, and competition?

Self-Care: The First Step to Divine Connection
While it's a buzzword that gets thrown around, the actual practice of self-care is frequently sidelined, dismissed as a luxury or even viewed with guilt as an act of selfishness. However, self-care is far from self-indulgent; it's a fundamental human need that serves as the foundation for any balanced, fulfilling relationship and life. The first step to connecting with the Divine Feminine within and around us is to honour ourselves. This means tuning into our own needs, both

physical and emotional, and giving ourselves permission to meet them. Whether it's taking time to meditate, indulging in a hobby, or simply getting enough sleep, these acts of self-care are essential for our well-being. The permission to prioritise self-care is a crucial element that many overlook. It's not just about finding the time; it's about giving ourselves the emotional clearance to say, "I matter. My well-being is important." This is especially vital for parents who find their own self-care at the bottom of their long list of jobs or in some cases not on the list at all. The aeroplane safety metaphor of putting on your own oxygen mask before assisting others is spot-on. If you're not at your best, how can you possibly offer the best to your partner or children?

Confidence is undeniably attractive, and nothing builds confidence like genuinely loving and taking care of yourself. Think about it: would you want to date someone who neglects themselves, who doesn't value their own well-being? Probably not. So why should your partner? Even in a long-term relationship or marriage, you're essentially still 'dating.' Keeping the spark alive involves maintaining yourself—not just for your partner but primarily for you.

The importance of self-care extends beyond individual wellness; it has a direct impact on the quality of our relationships. When we are well-cared for and our cup is full, we can engage more fully and lovingly with our partner. It eliminates the breeding ground for resentment, which often arises when we neglect our own needs in the service of meeting someone else's. For example, I make it a point to prioritise my meditation practice and exercise routine, not as an afterthought, but as a non-negotiable part of my day. I also make an effort to shave my legs every night before bed. It's not just about the act itself but what it represents: a commitment to maintaining both the emotional and physical aspects of my relationship with my husband.

Consistency is key here. Occasional acts of self-care are not enough to sustain us; it needs to be an ongoing commitment. Remember, you are the primary custodian of your own happiness. It's unfair and unrealistic to place the burden of your well-being solely on your partner's shoulders. When you take responsibility for your own happiness, you're not just doing yourself a favour; you're also enriching your relationship. By meeting your own needs, you're better equipped to meet your partner's needs, creating a virtuous cycle that leads to a balanced, healthy, and fulfilling relationship for both.

Meditation and Reflection: The Inner Sanctuary
The concept of an inner sanctuary is deeply rooted in ancient traditions, serving as a space for meditation, reflection, and connection with higher wisdom. In

ancient Greece, the Oracle at Delphi was more than just a figurehead; she was a priestess who served as a conduit for divine wisdom and guidance. Her role was to connect with the Divine Feminine through deep contemplation and meditation, providing insights that would guide individuals and even entire civilisations.

Today the need for such an inner sanctuary has never been greater. Amid the noise and distractions of modern life, it's easy to lose touch with our inner wisdom and intuition. Creating a dedicated space for stillness and reflection can serve as your modern-day Oracle, a place where you can connect with your innermost thoughts and feelings.

This doesn't necessarily mean you need a physical space—although setting up a meditation corner can certainly enhance the experience. The inner sanctuary is more about carving out time and mental space. Whether it's through meditation, journaling, or simply sitting in quiet contemplation, the goal is to tune into your intuition and listen to the wisdom that arises. Engaging in regular meditation and reflection allows you to tap into the Divine Feminine within, offering a wellspring of insights and guidance. This practice can help you navigate the complexities of modern life, from relationship challenges to career decisions, with a greater sense of clarity and purpose. It's about more than just problem-solving; it's a way to align yourself with your core values and deepest desires.

The act of entering this inner sanctuary is a ritual in itself, a sacred act that honours the Divine Feminine within you. It serves as a reminder that you are not alone; you are supported by a lineage of wisdom that stretches back through the ages. By making this practice a regular part of your routine, you're not just enhancing your own well-being; you're also strengthening your relationship by becoming a more centred, intuitive partner. So, take the time to create your own inner sanctuary. Make it a ritual, a non-negotiable part of your routine. As you connect with your inner wisdom, you'll find that you're not only gaining insights into your own life but also becoming a conduit for wisdom and balance in your relationships and your broader community.

Nature Connection: The Earthly Bond
The concept of connecting with nature as a way to balance and harmonise energies in a relationship is deeply rooted in indigenous cultures around the world. These ancient societies recognised the Earth as not just a resource but a living entity, a manifestation of the Divine Feminine that nurtures and sustains all life. They honoured this connection through various rituals and practices, from ceremonies to give thanks to the Earth to spending time in nature to connect with its energies.

Spending time in nature together can serve as a powerful ritual for modern couples. Whether it's a hike through the woods, a day at the beach, or even a simple walk in a local park, these moments allow you to disconnect from the digital world and reconnect with each other and the Earth. Feel the soil beneath your feet, listen to the rustle of leaves in the wind, and watch the sun dip below the horizon—these simple acts can have a profound impact on your well-being and the health of your relationship. As you absorb the nurturing energy of the Earth, you'll find yourselves more grounded, both as individuals and as a couple. This grounding effect can help you navigate the ups and downs of your relationship with greater equanimity. It can also deepen your emotional connection, as you share these sacred moments of peace and beauty.

This practice can serve as a reminder of your place in the larger web of life. It creates a sense of humility and gratitude, qualities that can enrich your relationship and your life in general. It's a way to step out of your individual and collective egos and recognise the interconnectedness of all things. So, make it a point to incorporate nature connection into your routine. It could be a weekly walk, a monthly camping trip, or even a yearly retreat to a remote natural location. Whatever form it takes, let this ritual serve as a touchstone for your relationship, a way to honour the

Divine Feminine within and around you, and a means to bring balance and harmony into your lives.

Express Creatively: The Dance of the Soul

The act of creative expression is deeply rooted in the Divine Feminine, a force that embodies creation, intuition, and emotional depth. Across various cultures and shamanic traditions, art and dance have been revered not just as forms of entertainment but as sacred practices that connect us to higher realms of consciousness. These acts of creation are often dedicated to goddesses and female spirits, acknowledging the Divine Feminine as the ultimate source of creative energy.

In today's fast-paced, logical world, we often neglect this creative aspect of ourselves. We get caught up in the day-to-day grind, focusing on tasks and responsibilities, and forget the nourishing power of creative expression. However, tapping into this creative energy can serve as a powerful ritual for modern couples, offering a unique pathway to balance and harmony. Whether it's painting a canvas, writing a poem, dancing in your living room, or even cooking a new recipe together, the act of creating something as a couple can be incredibly bonding. It allows you both to tap into a different part of yourselves, a part that is often overshadowed by the demands of modern life.

This is your chance to let your soul speak, to let your inner selves dance in the joy of creation.

As you engage in this creative process, you'll find yourselves connecting on a deeper level. The act of creating something together requires open communication, mutual respect, and a shared vision—key ingredients for any successful relationship.

Moreover, the energy you invest in this creative endeavour serves to enrich your relationship, adding a layer of depth and understanding that can be achieved in a few other ways. But the benefits don't stop there. Creative expression also serves as a form of emotional release, a way to process and make sense of the complexities of your inner world. It can serve as a form of therapy, a way to work through challenges and conflicts in a non-confrontational manner. As you each bring your unique skills and perspectives to the table, you're also learning to balance your individual energies, creating a harmonious blend of masculine and feminine forces. So, make room in your lives for creative expression. Set aside time each week to engage in a creative activity together. Let this become a sacred ritual, a time to disconnect from the outside world and connect with each other and the Divine Feminine that resides within you both. As you do, you'll find that this simple act serves as a powerful tool for balancing energies, enriching your relationship, and nourishing your soul.

Build a Community: The Circle of Support
Creating a sense of community is an essential aspect of embracing the Divine Feminine and balancing energies within your relationship. In many matriarchal societies, the community is essential, reflecting the Divine Feminine's values of collaboration, unity, and mutual support. The idea is simple yet profound: by surrounding yourself with a circle of supportive, understanding, and nurturing individuals, you create an environment that allows for growth, emotional well-being, and a balanced relationship.

Adding another layer to this is the concept of gender-specific circles, such as women's circles and men's circles. These circles offer a unique space to delve deeper into the energies that define us. I personally facilitate these circles and can attest to the transformative power they hold. The sense of community shared experiences, and the collective energy in these circles often lead to significant personal growth and emotional breakthroughs.

In a women's circle, the focus often shifts towards the Divine Feminine, exploring intuition, emotional intelligence, and nurturing. It's a sanctuary where women can openly share their experiences, challenges, and triumphs, learning from each other in a safe and supportive environment. The collective feminine energy in the room amplifies individual experiences, often leading to profound insights.

On the other hand, a men's circle offers a much-needed forum for exploring aspects of masculinity that are often overlooked or stigmatised. Topics like vulnerability, emotional expression, and the intricate balance between strength and sensitivity are explored. The collective masculine energy serves to elevate each man's understanding of what it means to be a balanced, emotionally intelligent individual in today's complex world. These circles are not just platforms for discussing challenges; they're also spaces for celebrating successes, sharing wisdom, and offering emotional support. They act as mirrors, reflecting both your strengths and areas for growth, empowering you to become a better version of yourself. The insights gained from these circles can be brought back into your relationship, enriching both your personal life and your partnership. So, if you're seeking to deepen your understanding of your own energy or aiming to balance the energies within your relationship participating in a gender-specific circle can be incredibly enlightening. These circles serve as a microcosm of the larger community, embodying the Divine Feminine's values of collaboration, unity, and mutual support, and they offer invaluable perspectives that can enrich both your life and your relationship.

The Divine Feminine is not just a relic of ancient myths and bygone civilisations. She is a vital, living force that beckons us to find balance in our lives, to respect the cyclical nature of existence, and to recognise the strength in vulnerability and the wisdom in intuition. By embracing her power and grace, we not only elevate our personal experiences but we can also bring healing, understanding, and compassion to our world—a world that deeply needs the gentle touch of the Divine Feminine.

Chapter 4 Honouring the Divine Masculine

From the dawn of civilisation, the masculine archetype has been a mainstay of human culture and spirituality. Whether it's the Norse myths of Odin, the Greek legends of Hercules, or the Native American stories of the Great Spirit, this archetype has been revered as a protector, a provider, and a leader. However, as societies evolved, the perception of this archetype became oversimplified, often reducing masculinity to mere physical prowess and emotional stoicism. This chapter aims to explore the multi-faceted nature of the Divine Masculine, how it has been honoured in ancient times, and how embracing it today can bring balance to ourselves and our romantic relationships.

Historically, the warrior was seen as an unyielding figure, steadfast in battle and emotionally composed. This stoicism became a sought-after quality, leading generations of men to believe that showing emotion was a sign of weakness. This perception has been passed down through the ages, from the Spartans of ancient Greece to the samurai of feudal Japan, and even to the modern military. While stoicism has its merits, such as teaching self-discipline and resilience, it became problematic when it suppressed the holistic expression of masculinity. The heroes of old were not just physical specimens; they were also thinkers, poets, and philosophers. They understood the complexities of the human condition, including pain, loss, and doubt. For example, King David of the Bible was not only a warrior but also a poet and musician. His Psalms are filled with expressions of deep emotional and spiritual experiences. Similarly, the Bhagavad Gita, a 700-verse Hindu scripture, is a conversation between Prince Arjuna and the god Krishna, who serves as his charioteer. In this dialogue, Arjuna is taught the importance of duty (Dharma) and righteousness, but also the value of compassion and moral integrity.

Today, the narrative around masculinity is changing. Researchers and thought leaders like Brené Brown have shown that vulnerability is not a weakness but a source of strength, creativity, and change. The modern masculine warrior is expected to be both sensitive and strong, aligning more closely with the ancient archetype where vulnerability becomes a source of power. In the realm of psychology, Carl Jung introduced the concept of anima and animus, suggesting that every man has a feminine side (anima) and every woman has a masculine side (animus). By integrating these aspects, individuals can achieve a more balanced personality. This idea has been further explored in modern psychology, where it's now understood that emotional intelligence—a blend of self-awareness, self-regulation, motivation, empathy, and social skills—is as important as cognitive intelligence.

Yet men have been historically discouraged from expressing "weaker" emotions like sadness or fear. This cultural conditioning has had a devastating impact on men's mental health. According to statistics, approximately 80% of suicides are men, a staggering figure that underscores the urgency of addressing this issue. The suppression of emotional expression not only affects individual men but also has a ripple effect on their relationships and the broader society. However, emotional expression is cathartic and healing. It creates deeper connections in romantic relationships and leads to genuine self-understanding. In ancient times tribal communities often had rituals and ceremonies that allowed men to express a range of emotions. These were considered rites of passage and were crucial for the emotional and psychological development of young men. For example, among the Maasai tribes in Africa, young men undergo a series of rites that include not only tests of physical endurance but also emotional and psychological training. They are taught the values of courage, but also compassion; strength, but also sensitivity. Similarly, in Native American cultures, vision quests and other rites of passage serve as both a physical and emotional journey, teaching young men the balance between bravery and wisdom, action and introspection.

In the context of romantic relationships, the ability for men to express their emotions freely adds a layer of depth and authenticity. It allows for a more balanced dynamic, where both partners can be vulnerable, open, and fully present with each other. This balance of the Divine Masculine's strength and action with the Divine Feminine's empathy and emotional intelligence creates a harmonious relationship that is resilient in the face of life's challenges.

So what are the characteristics of the Divine Masculine?

Strength and Courage
The attribute of "Strength and Courage" within the Divine Masculine is a nuanced and multi-dimensional concept that transcends mere physical might. In this framework physical strength is not about brute force or domination, but rather about using our physical abilities responsibly to protect and provide a safe space for others. This is a form of strength that aims to uplift rather than subjugate. Complementing physical strength is emotional resilience which allows for the full experience of life's emotional spectrum without being overwhelmed. This emotional strength is not just about self-reliance,
 but also about being a pillar of emotional support for others. It takes immense courage to be emotionally open, facing both joy and pain with grace. Spiritual

strength, another facet, is rooted in a sense of higher purpose or calling, providing the resilience to navigate life's complexities with integrity and alignment with our core values. Courage serves as the active manifestation of all forms of strength enabling one to confront challenges and fears head-on while maintaining ethical integrity. In the Divine Masculine courage and strength are not exercised recklessly, but are grounded in a strong ethical framework ensuring they are wielded wisely and justly. Overall, "Strength and Courage" encapsulates physical, emotional and spiritual fortitude, all courageously applied in a manner that is in harmony with our deepest values and respects the well-being of others.

Leadership and responsibility
Leadership and Responsibility are not just key attributes of the Divine Masculine they are transformative principles that challenge traditional or patriarchal notions often associated with these terms. Unlike conventional models that may emphasise control, domination, or authoritarianism, the Divine Masculine redefines leadership as an exercise in wisdom, discernment, and collaboration. This enlightened form of leadership is not about dictating terms or imposing will, but about guiding through wisdom and empowering others to reach their full potential. It's a consultative approach that values the

input and perspectives of others aiming to arrive at holistic solutions that benefit everyone involved.

Responsibility, in this framework, is equally groundbreaking. The Divine Masculine recognises that every action, word and decision has consequences, not just for oneself, but for the broader community, environment and even the world. This is a form of responsibility that goes beyond mere accountability, it's born out of a deep sense of ethical integrity and a commitment to doing what is right, even when it's challenging or inconvenient. It's about being responsible not just for oneself, but for the well-being of others, understanding that individual actions contribute to collective outcomes.

When applied to the context of romantic relationships and family life, these attributes take on even deeper significance. Leadership becomes a partnership based on mutual respect and shared decision-making where both partners contribute to the well-being of the relationship and family. Responsibility extends to being a role model for children demonstrating through action what it means to be a compassionate, strong, and ethical individual. It's about making choices that are aligned with shared family values and taking responsibility for the emotional and physical well-being of the family as a whole.

The Divine Masculine's approach to leadership and responsibility is a harmonious blend of strength and humility, authority and empathy, decisiveness and wisdom. It's an approach that seeks not just to lead. but to elevate, not just to be responsible, but to be ethically and morally grounded. In doing so, it aims to create environments, be it in relationships, families, or communities, that are balanced, harmonious, and just.

Rational and Logic

The Divine Masculine embodies a unique blend of intellectual attributes among which rationality and logic hold a special place. Unlike a cold detached form of reasoning the Divine Masculine's approach to rationality is deeply rooted in wisdom and ethical considerations. It's not just about dissecting problems into manageable parts, but about understanding the broader implications of each decision. This form of logical thinking is both analytical and holistic, capable of zooming in on the details while never losing sight of the bigger picture. It's a balanced form of intellect that combines the analytical mind with intuitive insights, creating a well-rounded approach to problem-solving. This rationality extends to the ability to create structure and order, not as a means of control, but as a way to cultivate a harmonious environment where everyone can thrive. Whether it's in the workplace, at home, or in personal relationships, this attribute manifests as thoughtful organisation, clear communication, and the establishment of fair and just systems. In essence, the Divine Masculine's approach to rationality and logic is not an end in itself but a tool for creating a more balanced, equitable, and thoughtful world.

Focus and Determination
The attributes of focus and determination take on a special significance within the context of romantic relationships. In the Divine Masculine focus is not merely a spotlight on individual goals or ambitions; it's also a concentrated attention on the needs, desires and emotional well-being of a partner. This focus creates a nurturing space for the relationship to flourish where both partners feel seen, heard and valued. Determination, too, evolves within the romantic sphere. It's not just about personal perseverance, but also embodies a steadfast commitment to the relationship itself. This means working through challenges together, maintaining the integrity of the partnership even when times are tough and continually investing in mutual growth and happiness.

In a romantic relationship, this blend of focus and determination serves as the backbone for long-term commitment and emotional intimacy. It's about having the clarity to know what the relationship needs to thrive and the resolve to put in the work to make it happen. This isn't a rigid or dogmatic approach, but one that's adaptable and responsive to the ever-changing dynamics between two individuals. It's about being attuned not just to our own needs, but also to the needs of the partner and the relationship as a whole. In this way, the Divine Masculine's focus and determination contribute to a balanced fulfilling partnership that stands the test of time, enriching both individuals and creating a harmonious union.

Protection and Provision
The Divine Masculine's protective nature serves as a sanctuary of strength and security, creating a safe space where both partners can grow and thrive. This isn't just about physical safety, but also emotional and spiritual well-being. It's about providing a stable foundation upon which the relationship can flourish, whether that means offering emotional support, sharing wisdom, or contributing to material needs. This attribute of protection and provision takes on a nuanced complementary role in a balanced relationship with the Divine Feminine.

The Divine Masculine's focus on external provision and protection complements the Divine Feminine's internal, emotional, and spiritual nurturing. She brings a different, but equally important form of protection, often likened to that of a nurturing, protective mother. This energy is not just about shielding from external harm, but also about enabling internal growth, emotional intelligence and spiritual depth. Together, they create a holistic environment where both partners feel secure and supported, both in their individual pursuits and within the relationship itself. This balanced dynamic allows for a relationship that is not just safe and provided for, but also emotionally rich and spiritually fulfilling.

Emotional Stability

Emotional stability, a key attribute of the Divine Masculine, is essential not just for individual well-being, but also for the health of relationships, families, and even broader communities. While fully in touch with his emotions the Divine Masculine possesses the unique ability not to be controlled by them. This isn't about emotional detachment, but rather about a balanced approach to emotional expression and management. He offers a form of emotional strength that becomes a grounding force in relationships, providing a stable foundation upon which trust, understanding, and intimacy can be built.

In the context of family, this emotional stability is invaluable. It creates a secure environment where each family member, adult or child, feels safe to express themselves emotionally. Children, in particular, benefit from this stability, learning early on the importance of emotional intelligence and how to navigate their own feelings without being overwhelmed by them. The ripple effect of this emotional stability extends even further, impacting the larger community. A person who embodies the Divine Masculine's emotional stability is likely to be a source of strength and support in wider social circles, workplaces, and community organisations. They bring a sense of calm and rationality in emotionally charged situations, helping to resolve conflicts and build a more harmonious coexistence. In essence, the emotional stability inherent in the Divine Masculine is not just a personal asset, it's a communal one, contributing to the emotional and psychological well-being of everyone within that community.

Integrity and Authenticity
Integrity and authenticity are foundational attributes of the Divine Masculine, serving as guiding principles in both personal and interpersonal dynamics. Integrity is manifested through a steadfast commitment to ethical behaviour, a consistency between words and actions, and a deep alignment with our core values. It's not merely about following a moral code, but about embodying it in every decision and interaction. This integrity becomes the bedrock of trust in relationships, whether romantic, familial, or communal. Authenticity complements this by emphasising the importance of being true to oneself. It rejects the notion of conforming to societal or external expectations that

are at odds with our own beliefs, needs, or values. In a romantic relationship, this authenticity allows for a deeper emotional connection, as each partner feels safe to be their true selves, unmasked and unfiltered. In a family setting parents who embody these traits serve as powerful role models for their children, teaching them the importance of honesty, respect, and self-respect. Moreover, in a community, individuals who exemplify integrity and authenticity contribute to a culture of transparency, accountability and mutual respect. In essence integrity and authenticity are not just personal virtues, but collective assets that enrich relationships, fortify families and strengthen communities.

Wisdom and Insight
Wisdom and insight are quintessential traits of the Divine Masculine embodying a depth of understanding that transcends mere knowledge. This wisdom is not an accidental byproduct but is cultivated through years of experience, introspection and a profound engagement with both the inner self and the external world. It's about making sense of complexities, discerning the subtle nuances in situations, and offering insights that bring clarity and resolution. In the context of relationships, this wisdom becomes invaluable. A partner who embodies these traits can navigate the intricacies of emotional dynamics, offering a stabilising influence when

conflicts arise. They bring a long-term perspective to issues, seeing beyond immediate challenges to the larger picture. Within a family a parent with such wisdom can guide their children through life's complexities, offering counsel that is both practical and deeply insightful. This wisdom also extends to community interactions, where it contributes to a more harmonious coexistence. The Divine Masculine's wisdom and insight offer a complementary balance to the intuitive nurturing aspects of the Divine Feminine, creating a holistic approach to problem-solving, relationship-building, and personal growth. Together they form a balanced yin-yang dynamic that enriches every facet of life.

Compassion and Understanding
Compassion and understanding, although frequently attributed to the Divine Feminine, are equally vital components of the Divine Masculine. In a balanced individual, these traits manifest as a deep sense of empathy not just for your partner, family, or community, but also for yourself. This self-compassion is crucial because it forms the basis for extending genuine compassion to others. In the context of romantic relationships, a partner who embodies the Divine Masculine's compassion and understanding can deeply enrich the emotional landscape of the relationship. They are attuned to their partner's needs, responsive rather than reactive and capable of holding

space for their partner's emotions without judgement. This creates a nurturing environment where both partners feel seen, heard and valued. When balanced with the intuitive and nurturing qualities of the Divine Feminine, this compassionate aspect of the Divine Masculine contributes to a harmonious and deeply fulfilling relationship. Together, they create a partnership where both emotional and rational faculties are engaged, where both partners feel supported and empowered, and where the relationship itself becomes a sanctuary of mutual respect, love and understanding.

Humility
Humility is a defining attribute of the Divine Masculine serving as a grounding force amidst his many strengths and capabilities. This humility is not a sign of weakness, but rather an acknowledgment of being part of something larger. It reflects an openness to learning, growing and evolving, both as an individual and in relation to others. In the context of relationships and family life, this humility allows for a more balanced and harmonious dynamic. It creates space for the partner's voice and wisdom creating a relationship built on mutual respect rather than ego-driven power dynamics. When paired with the nurturing and intuitive qualities of the Divine Feminine, this humility contributes to a balanced, holistic approach to life and relationships. It allows for a partnership where both

individuals can flourish, continually learning from each other and from the experiences that life brings their way. Understanding and integrating this sense of humility is not just beneficial for men but for anyone seeking a more balanced existence. Both the Divine Masculine and Divine Feminine energies exist within all of us, irrespective of our gender and achieving a balance between these energies is often seen as a pathway to a more fulfilled, harmonious life.

The journey toward embracing the Divine Masculine is multi-faceted, involving both internal and external practices. So how do we cultivate these energies in today's world:

Self-awareness and Introspection
Self-awareness and introspection are foundational elements in embracing the Divine Masculine within. Unlike the outward focus that often characterises our busy lives, introspection calls for a turning inward, a deep dive into the self to explore our fears, dreams, insecurities, and aspirations. This is not a one-time exercise but an ongoing practice that requires commitment and sincerity. The ancient Stoics, for example, had a form of journaling known as 'Meditations,' a practice that involved daily reflection on our actions, thoughts, and feelings. The aim was not just to record these observations but to scrutinise them, to understand the motivations behind them,

and to use this understanding as a tool for self-improvement and personal growth. This Stoic practice aligns well with the Divine Masculine's emphasis on self-awareness, responsibility, and purposeful action. In modern relationships, this level of self-awareness can be transformative. When you understand your own triggers, desires, and emotional patterns, you're better equipped to navigate the complexities of a partnership. It allows for more effective communication, as you're able to articulate your needs and understandings clearly. It also nurtures emotional intelligence, enabling you to empathise with your partner's perspective, even if it differs from your own.

Journaling is one effective way to cultivate this self-awareness. Regularly putting your thoughts and feelings down on paper can offer surprising insights into your own psyche. It serves as a mirror, reflecting both your strengths and your vulnerabilities. Reflective meditation is another powerful tool. Unlike other forms of meditation that focus on emptying the mind or concentrating on a particular object, reflective meditation encourages you to explore your thoughts and feelings, to sit with them without judgement, and to gain insights that can lead to personal growth. However, the benefits of self-awareness and introspection extend beyond the individual and the relationship. When you're in tune with your inner self, you're more likely to engage with the world around you in a meaningful way. You become more conscious of your actions and their impact on others, leading to more responsible and ethical choices. In essence, the Divine Masculine's call for self-awareness is not just a call for individual betterment but for the betterment of society as a whole.

In conclusion, self-awareness and introspection are not just self-help buzzwords but vital practices that tap into the essence of the Divine Masculine. By making them a regular part of your life, you set the stage for deeper understanding, more fulfilling relationships, and a more purposeful existence.

Safe Spaces for Emotional Expression
Safe Spaces for Emotional Expression are more than just a modern-day concept; they are a fundamental need for human growth and connection. The Divine Masculine, often misconstrued as stoic or emotionally reserved, actually thrives in environments where emotional expression is encouraged and respected. This is not a departure from strength but an extension of it. True strength lies in the ability to be vulnerable, to express our feelings openly, and to engage in genuine self-examination.

Creating such spaces can take various forms. It could be a men's group where topics often considered "taboo" are openly discussed, allowing for a deeper exploration of the masculine psyche. It could be a therapy session, where guided professional support offers a structured environment for emotional unpacking. Or it could be as simple as open, judgement-free conversations with loved ones, where the floor is open for any topic, no matter how sensitive. The benefits of these safe spaces are manifold. First and foremost, they offer a cathartic release, a way to unload emotional burdens that may have been carried for days, months, or even years. This emotional unburdening is not just good for mental health; it's also physically beneficial, as emotional stress often manifests in physical ailments.

Secondly, these spaces enable deeper connections in romantic relationships. When both partners feel safe enough to express their deepest fears, joys, and dreams, it creates a level of intimacy that surface-level conversations can never achieve. It's the difference between knowing someone and truly understanding them. This emotional intimacy serves as the bedrock for a strong, resilient relationship that can weather the inevitable storms of life.

Lastly, safe spaces for emotional expression lead to genuine self-understanding. When you articulate your feelings, you're also forced to confront them—to understand their origins, their impact, and their implications for your life. This self-understanding is invaluable, as it guides your actions and decisions, helping you live a life more aligned with your true self.

In a world that often prioritises action over reflection, and output over emotion, creating safe spaces for emotional expression is a revolutionary act. It's a commitment to the wholeness of human experience, an acknowledgement that our emotional selves are as real and as important as our physical and intellectual selves. By prioritising emotional expression, we not only enrich our own lives but also contribute to a more compassionate, empathetic, and emotionally intelligent society.

Empathy: The Heart of Emotional Connection
Empathy is often hailed as a pillar of the Divine Feminine, but it's equally vital in the realm of the Divine Masculine. Contrary to the stereotype of the stoic, emotionally detached male figure, true masculine strength lies in the ability to be empathetic and to understand and share the feelings of others. This is a form of emotional intelligence that transcends gender and taps into the core of what it means to be human.

In romantic relationships, empathy serves as a powerful catalyst for deeper emotional connection. It's the ability to put yourself in your partner's shoes, to feel what they feel, and to offer emotional support or practical solutions, as needed. This creates a safe space where both partners can be vulnerable, leading to a more authentic and fulfilling relationship.

The value of empathy isn't just a modern discovery; it's a timeless truth acknowledged by many ancient cultures. Leaders in these societies were often chosen not just for their physical strength or strategic acumen but for their ability to understand and connect with their people. In Native American tribes, for example, chiefs were often those who demonstrated great wisdom and empathy. Similarly, in ancient Chinese philosophy, the ideal ruler was described as one who had a deep emotional connection with his subjects, understanding their needs and worries.
Empathy is not a sign of weakness but a hallmark of true strength. It requires the courage to be vulnerable, and to open oneself up to the full spectrum of human emotion. And in doing so, it allows us to forge deeper connections, not just with our romantic partners, but with everyone around us. It's a skill that enriches our lives, enhances our relationships, and, ultimately, makes us better, more balanced human beings.

Mindfulness and Self-Awareness: The Pillars of Emotional Well-Being
While awareness around mental health is growing, it's crucial to note that men are still disproportionately affected by issues like depression and suicide. Making

it imperative to address emotional well-being as a vital aspect of the Divine Masculine.

Mindfulness and self-awareness practices offer a powerful toolkit for improving mental health and emotional balance. Rooted in Buddhist philosophy, these techniques, such as focused breathing, meditation, and mindful walking, serve as a gateway to understanding our emotional landscape. By becoming aware of your thoughts, feelings, and reactions, you're better equipped to manage your emotional state, thereby embracing vulnerability in a healthy way. The practice of mindfulness is not just about moment-to-moment awareness but also about cultivating a deeper understanding of oneself. This introspective journey can be transformative, especially for men who have been socially conditioned to suppress their emotions. By breaking down these barriers, mindfulness paves the way for greater empathy, improved relationships, and a more balanced life.

The ripple effects of mindfulness and self-awareness are profound. They not only improve your own mental health but also positively impact those around you. In romantic relationships, for instance, being emotionally aware and present can lead to deeper connections and better communication. In a broader societal context, men who are emotionally balanced contribute to breaking down the stigmas surrounding mental health, thereby encouraging other men to seek help and engage in self-care.

Artistic Engagement: The Renaissance of the Modern Man

The notion of artistic engagement as a pathway to emotional and intellectual enrichment has deep historical roots. During the Renaissance in Italy, the concept of the "Renaissance Man" emerged as an ideal. This was a man proficient not just in sciences and social graces but also deeply engaged in the arts. Whether it was painting like Leonardo da Vinci, sculpting like Michelangelo, or writing like Petrarch, the arts were considered not just hobbies but essential aspects of a well-rounded individual. This ideal form of masculinity celebrated a balance between logical reasoning and emotional expression, between the sciences and the arts.

In today's context, the value of artistic engagement remains just as relevant, especially for men seeking to embrace a balanced form of masculinity. Engaging in artistic activities—be it painting, writing, music, or even the simple act of appreciating art—serves as a conduit for emotional expression. It offers a safe space to explore one's feelings, thoughts, and even fears, providing a form of emotional release that many men find difficult to achieve otherwise. But the benefits extend beyond emotional catharsis. Artistic engagement also enables self-awareness and introspection. As you create or appreciate art, you're compelled to delve into your own psyche, to understand the motivations behind your artistic choices or preferences. This can lead to profound insights into your own character, helping you understand yourself better.

The act of creating art can be a shared experience, offering a unique opportunity for emotional connection with a partner or loved ones. It can serve as a mutual journey of discovery, where both parties learn not just about each other but also about themselves. This shared artistic endeavour can strengthen relationships, providing a new layer of emotional depth and understanding.

In a world that often prioritises logic and reason over emotional intelligence, artistic engagement serves as a reminder of the value of balance. It encourages men to embrace a more holistic form of masculinity—one that celebrates emotional expression and self-awareness as much as strength and resilience. By engaging with the arts, modern men can take a page from the Renaissance playbook, striving for a balanced, well-rounded life that enriches both themselves and those around them.

Educating the Next Generation: Building Foundations for Balanced Relationships

The importance of emotional intelligence and balance cannot be overstated, especially when it comes to educating the next generation of men. In a society that often equates masculinity with emotional stoicism, teaching young men that it's okay to be emotional and that their feelings are valid is not just progressive—it's imperative for their well-being and for the health of their future relationships.

Why this is not taught in school is beyond me and a change I hope to see in my lifetime. In my opinion Schools and community programs should consider integrating emotional intelligence training into their curricular. This could take various forms, from workshops and seminars to ongoing educational courses. The aim is to equip young men with the tools they need to understand and manage their emotions, thereby creating healthier interpersonal relationships. Given the absence of this element in our education system, it becomes even more crucial for us to embrace and nurture the Divine Masculine within ourselves, our relationships, and our community.

In many indigenous cultures storytelling is a revered practice used to pass down wisdom from one generation to the next. These stories often encapsulate lessons on emotional balance, strength, and the importance of community. Incorporating such storytelling methods into modern educational programs could serve as a culturally rich and engaging way to impart these crucial life skills.

The benefits of such educational initiatives extend far beyond the individual. When men are taught to embrace their emotional selves, they become better equipped to engage in balanced, fulfilling relationships. They become better listeners, more empathetic partners, and more emotionally available—qualities that enrich not just romantic relationships but all interpersonal interactions.

Women, too, stand to gain from a societal shift that encourages the balance of Divine Masculine and Feminine energies. In a relationship where both partners are emotionally intelligent and balanced, the dynamic becomes incredibly empowering. Both individuals are emotionally available, deeply connected, and mutually respectful, creating a relationship that transcends mere romantic love to become spiritually enriching.

The implementation of educational programs that focus on emotional intelligence and balance is not just beneficial but essential for nurturing healthier individuals and relationships. By laying this foundation for the next generation, we set the stage for more harmonious, respectful, and deeply connected unions in the future.

By educating and integrating these practices into daily life, men can reclaim the full spectrum of the Divine Masculine, moving beyond outdated stereotypes and embracing a balanced, holistic form of masculinity. This is not just beneficial for men but for everyone they interact with, creating a ripple effect that can lead to more balanced, respectful, and harmonious relationships and communities.

Chapter 5: Balancing the Energies

In the intricate dance of life, the Divine Feminine and Divine Masculine energies play pivotal roles. These energies are not confined to gender; they are universal forces that exist within each of us. In a romantic relationship, achieving a balance between these energies can lead to a harmonious, fulfilling, and deeply connected union.

The concept of balancing masculine and feminine energies is not new. Ancient civilisations had a profound understanding of these energies and their importance in relationships.

The ancient wisdom surrounding the balance of masculine and feminine energies has been deeply understood and revered by civilisations throughout history. In Taoism, the well-known concept of Yin and Yang serves as a foundational example. Yin, representing the Feminine, and Yang, representing the Masculine, are seen as complementary forces whose balance is essential for harmony. This equilibrium is particularly crucial in relationships, where it creates mutual respect and emotional well-being. Similarly, in Hinduism, the divine couple of Shiva and Shakti epitomises this perfect balance. Shiva, embodying the Divine Masculine, is seen as the destroyer and the transformer, while Shakti, representing the Divine Feminine, is considered the source of all energy. Their cosmic union is often held as the ultimate expression of love and universal energy. Even in Greek mythology, the union of Zeus and Hera, despite its complexities, symbolises a balance between power and nurturing, a recurring theme that has been immortalised in myths and stories.

When it comes to creating fulfilling balanced relationships the importance of achieving a balance between the Divine Feminine and Divine Masculine energies in romantic relationships cannot be overstated. A balanced relationship paves the way for a deeper emotional connection, where both partners feel heard, respected, and valued, ultimately leading to a more fulfilling and stronger union. This equilibrium also enables mutual growth, allowing each of you to focus on personal development without overshadowing the other, resulting in a partnership where you both grow together rather than apart. In terms of communication, the balance is equally crucial. The Divine Feminine, often linked with emotional intelligence and communication, complements the Divine Masculine's attributes of action and decisiveness, ensuring that conversations are not only meaningful but also lead to constructive action. Furthermore, this balance extends to the realm of sexual intimacy, enhancing compatibility by harmonising the energies of giving and receiving, as well as leading and following, we have a whole chapter on that later. For now let's start with how to balance the energies in your relationship.

Embrace Vulnerability: The Samurai Way of Love
When it comes to balancing energies one key element is embracing vulnerability. The Samurai warriors of feudal Japan offer a compelling example of this. Known for their fierce fighting skills, they were also poets, artists, and philosophers. They understood that true strength came from a balanced character, one that could be as gentle as it was strong, as introspective as it was outward-focused.

In modern relationships, vulnerability often gets a bad rap, associated with weakness or emotional fragility making it difficult for us to express. However, vulnerability is actually a strength. It's the courage to show your true self, to let your partner see you—flaws, fears, dreams, and all. This openness creates a space for deep emotional connection, which is where the feminine energy of nurturing and understanding can flourish.

To embrace vulnerability, create a 'safe space' within your relationship where both partners can freely express their thoughts, feelings, and fears without judgement. This could be a specific time you set aside each week or a physical space like a favourite spot in your home. The idea is to create an environment where both masculine and feminine energies can be freely expressed and received.

Consider incorporating rituals that encourage vulnerability. For example, you might have a weekly 'heart-to-heart' session where you both share something you're grateful for, something you're struggling with, and something you're looking forward to. These rituals can serve as touchpoints, moments where you consciously set aside time to drop the masks and be truly present with each other.

Embracing vulnerability doesn't mean that one partner becomes 'the vulnerable one' while the other becomes 'the strong one.' Rather, it's about both partners taking turns in these roles, understanding that everyone has moments of strength and moments of vulnerability. This fluid exchange of energies creates a dynamic, balanced relationship. When you allow yourselves to be vulnerable, you're not just opening up emotionally. You're also paving the way for greater intimacy, trust, and mutual respect—qualities that enrich any relationship. You'll find that your communication improves, your emotional bonds deepen, and your understanding of each other becomes more nuanced. Embracing vulnerability is not a sign of weakness but a testament to the strength of your relationship. It's a conscious choice to show up authentically, allowing both masculine and feminine energies to coexist and enrich your shared life.

Nurturing and Protecting

In ancient tribes, the roles of nurturing and protecting were not confined to one gender. Men were not only protectors and providers but also nurturers who played an active role in the emotional and spiritual well-being of their communities. This holistic approach to caregiving created a balanced, harmonious society where both masculine and feminine energies were valued and utilised.

Fast forward to today, and we find that societal norms have unfairly labelled nurturing as a 'feminine' trait and protecting as a 'masculine' role. This division perpetuates gender stereotypes and deprives relationships of the richness that comes from embracing both energies. The truth is, that both partners in a relationship have the capacity to nurture and protect, and the most fulfilling relationships are those where these roles are fluid, shared, and mutually respected.

I feel for men today, the modern man finds himself at a crossroads where he's encouraged to be emotionally available, empathetic, and engaged in family life, while also maintaining the traditional roles of strength, resilience, and provision. This can be a challenging tightrope to walk, especially without the right tools and understanding to balance these energies effectively. A man who can be a strong provider but also emotionally present is not just an ideal but a necessity for the health of modern relationships and families.

Nurturing isn't just about caring for physical needs; it's also about emotional and intellectual nurturing. This could mean supporting each other's career ambitions, encouraging personal growth, or simply being there to listen and offer emotional support. It's about creating a safe space where both partners can thrive and grow. In a balanced relationship, both partners take turns playing the nurturer, providing emotional support and encouragement in different situations.

Protecting isn't solely about physical safety; it's also about safeguarding your shared dreams, goals, and values. This could involve standing up for your partner in social situations, or it could mean making sacrifices to achieve a shared long-term goal. Protection in this sense is a mutual endeavour, one that requires both partners to invest in the relationship's long-term health and happiness.

When men are balanced in their energies, it creates a ripple effect that benefits their relationships and families. A balanced man can be a rock for his partner while also being a wellspring of emotional support. He can be a role model for his children, teaching his sons that it's okay to be sensitive and showing his daughters that they deserve to be treated with respect and equality.

To help you do this, consider establishing rituals that honour both the nurturing and protecting aspects of your relationship. For example, you could have a monthly 'dreams and goals' discussion where you check in on your shared aspirations and strategise ways to achieve them. This serves the dual purpose of nurturing your shared vision while also protecting it through planning and mutual accountability. When both partners feel free to express their nurturing and protective sides, something magical happens. The relationship becomes a dynamic, balanced ecosystem where both individuals can flourish. Challenges are more easily overcome, joys are more profoundly shared, and the overall emotional health of the relationship is enhanced.

By embracing this balanced approach, we set the stage for more harmonious relationships, healthier families, and a more balanced society.

Fluid Roles
The ancient Mayans had a holistic view of masculine and feminine energies, seeing them as two sides of the same coin. In their society, these energies were not in opposition but were complementary, each bringing its own set of strengths and qualities to the table. This

perspective allowed for a more fluid, balanced approach to roles within relationships and the community.

In contrast, modern society often imposes rigid roles based on gender, creating limitations and imbalances. Men are frequently expected to be the primary breadwinners and problem-solvers, while women are often pigeonholed into caregiving and emotional support roles. These stereotypes can stifle individual growth and create tension in relationships, as they don't allow for the natural fluidity and balance of masculine and feminine energies.

Fluidity in roles means that responsibilities and tasks are not assigned based on gender but are instead divided based on individual strengths, preferences, and the needs of the relationship or situation. For example, if one partner is better at handling finances, they take on that role, regardless of whether it's traditionally considered a "man's" or "woman's" job. Similarly, if one partner is more emotionally intuitive, they might naturally take the lead in emotional caregiving, irrespective of their gender. Embracing fluid roles in a relationship offers a multitude of benefits that contribute to a more harmonious and fulfilling partnership. By leveraging each individual's unique strengths, couples can solve problems more effectively and enrich the overall quality of their relationship. This approach also alleviates the stress and tension that often arise from trying to conform to traditional, predefined roles. Furthermore, fluidity in roles creates a climate of equality and mutual respect, as it allows both partners to value each other's contributions, regardless of gender. Importantly, the process of discussing and negotiating these roles necessitates open and honest communication, thereby fortifying the relationship itself.

To implement fluid roles in your relationship, start by having an open discussion about your individual strengths, preferences, and the needs of your relationship. From there, you can collaboratively decide how to divide responsibilities in a way that honours both partners and enhances the relationship's overall well-being.

Embracing fluid roles in relationships is not a new concept but a timeless wisdom, deeply rooted in ancient cultures like the Mayans. By breaking free from the limitations of modern societal norms and adopting a more fluid, balanced approach, we pave the way for richer, more fulfilling relationships that honour the complete range of human experience and capability.

The Ancient Art of Speaking Truths
In ancient societies, open communication was revered as a blend of logic and intuition, each considered

essential for personal and communal well-being. Communication is so key to all relationships we have a whole chapter on it later, but for now let me just say that effective communication involves both logic, which provides structure and clarity, and intuition which allows for emotional nuance and deeper connection. Balanced communication serves as a powerful tool for conflict resolution, emotional bonding, personal growth, and trust-building.

Practical steps for achieving this balance include active listening, being mindful of non-verbal cues, and choosing the right time and setting for important conversations. By embracing this balanced approach, we can navigate modern relationship complexities with wisdom, just as our ancestors did.

Celebrate the Dance
In Hindu mythology, the cosmic dance of Shiva and Shakti represents the eternal interplay of masculine and feminine energies. Shiva, the destroyer and transformer, and Shakti, the divine feminine energy, are in a perpetual dance of creation, preservation, and destruction. This dance is not just a spectacle but a profound metaphor for the dynamic energies that exist within each of us and within our relationships.

In the modern context, this dance can be seen as the ever-changing dynamics between partners. There are moments of creation, where new experiences and memories are formed. There are periods of preservation, where the relationship enjoys stability and peace. And yes, there are times of destruction or transformation, when old patterns need to be broken for new growth to occur.

Celebrating this dance means embracing the full spectrum of experiences in your relationship. It's about acknowledging that there will be highs and lows, periods of intense passion and times of quiet companionship, challenges that test your resilience, and triumphs that elevate your love. Each phase, each shift, is a step in your ongoing dance, and recognising this can bring a sense of sacredness to your relationship.

To practically celebrate this dance, consider creating rituals or traditions that honour these different phases. For example, you could have a special celebration for relationship milestones (creation), regular check-ins or date nights to maintain your emotional connection (preservation), and perhaps even rituals for letting go of old grievances or habits that no longer serve you (destruction/transformation).

Dual Meditation
Meditation has long been a essential for spiritual and emotional well-being, and its benefits extend

beautifully into the realm of relationships. Dual meditation, where both partners meditate together, can be a transformative experience that not only deepens your individual self-awareness but also enhances the emotional and energetic connection between you and your partner.

The concept of dual meditation has roots in various ancient traditions, from Tantric practices to Taoist philosophies. These traditions understood the power of collective energy and the profound impact it could have on relationships. By meditating together, couples could align their energies, create a sense of unity and balance that transcended physical and emotional barriers.

In today's context, dual meditation can serve as a regular practice for couples aiming to balance their masculine and feminine energies. The practice involves sitting together in a quiet, comfortable space, free from distractions. You then engage in guided meditations that focus on visualising the masculine and feminine energies within each of you intertwining and harmonising.

Engaging in dual meditation offers a multitude of benefits that enrich your relationship in profound ways. As you both concentrate on harmonising your energies, you naturally become more attuned to each other's emotional states, deepening your emotional bond. This quiet, shared space often serves as a catalyst for more meaningful and honest communication, allowing you both to articulate your thoughts and feelings more clearly. Beyond emotional and communicative benefits, the calming effect of meditating together serves as a powerful stress reducer, enhancing your overall sense of contentment and happiness within the relationship. Furthermore, this focus on energetic balance also facilitates the alignment of your goals and values, streamlining the decision-making process and making it easier to navigate challenges as a united front.

Make it a weekly ritual, perhaps choosing a specific day and time to sit down together. You could even incorporate elements like candles or soft background music to enhance the experience. The key is consistency; the more regularly you practise dual meditation, the more you'll begin to see its positive effects ripple through your relationship.
In summary, dual meditation is more than just a trendy wellness practice; it's a powerful tool for couples looking to balance their masculine and feminine energies. By making this a regular part of your relationship ritual, you're investing in a deeper, more harmonious connection with your partner.

Be in nature
Being in nature serves as a powerful catalyst for harmonising the masculine and feminine energies within us. The natural world, with its intricate balance of strength and softness, activity and stillness, offers a perfect backdrop for couples seeking to align their energies. Beyond the metaphysical, nature also has a physiological impact on us. The release of dopamine and oxytocin during time spent outdoors puts us in a calmer, more receptive state, enhancing our clarity and understanding.

My husband and I have found this to be profoundly true in our own relationship. We make it a point to walk our dogs together in the beautiful countryside where we live every week. These walks are more than just exercise or a break from routine; they're our sanctuary. Away from the distractions of work, kids, and daily responsibilities, we find that our conversations flow. We discuss our dreams, our worries, our joys and laugh together all while surrounded by the tranquillity of nature. The act of walking side by side, in the fresh air, creates a space for us to connect on a deeper level. These regular nature walks have become a ritual for us, a sacred time to rejuvenate not just our individual selves but also our connection as a couple. We return from these walks feeling more aligned, both with ourselves and with each other, ready to face whatever challenges the coming week may bring. So, if you're looking to balance energies and deepen your relationship, consider making time for nature. It's a simple yet profoundly effective way to reconnect, recalibrate, and rejuvenate your love.

Artistic Expression
Artistic expression offers a unique platform for couples to explore and balance their masculine and feminine energies. Engaging in collaborative artistic projects allows you to play with these roles in a tangible way. For instance, one partner can take on the 'masculine' role of leading the project, setting the vision, and making key decisions, while the other adopts the 'feminine' role of nurturing the idea, adding details, and providing emotional and creative support. Once the project reaches a certain stage, you can then swap roles, allowing each partner to experience both the leading and nurturing aspects of creation.

This practice does more than just produce a piece of art; it serves as a microcosm of your relationship, a safe space to experiment with different roles and responsibilities. It also encourages a deeper understanding of each other's strengths and preferences, which can be invaluable in other areas of your relationship. For example, the partner who enjoys taking the lead in artistic endeavours might also be more comfortable taking charge in other situations, like planning trips or making financial decisions.

Conversely, the partner who excels at nurturing the artistic process might find fulfilment in supporting and enriching other aspects of your shared life.

Moreover, the act of creating something together is inherently unifying. It requires open communication, mutual respect, and a shared vision—key ingredients for any successful relationship. As you both contribute your unique skills and perspectives to the project, you're also contributing to a deeper, more balanced connection with each other. The finished artwork then becomes a symbol of your harmonised energies, a tangible reminder of what you can achieve when you work together in a balanced and respectful manner.

This was true of Linda and Robert, a couple in their early 50s who I worked with. They found themselves in a relationship rut until they rediscovered their shared passion for painting. This led them to set up a small art studio in their home, where they began to collaborate on various projects. As they painted, they found themselves talking more openly and honestly than they had in years. Over time, their art projects became a sacred ritual, a dedicated space to balance their masculine and feminine energies and reconnect on a deeper level.

So, whether it's painting a canvas, composing a song, building a piece of furniture, or any other creative endeavour, consider doing it together. It's not just an opportunity to express yourselves but also a powerful ritual for balancing energies and strengthening your relationship.

Sacred Circles
The practice of sitting together in a circle to share feelings and thoughts is a ritual deeply rooted in Native American traditions. Known for its power to build community and deepen relationships, this practice can be adapted for modern couples looking to balance their masculine and feminine energies.
In a Sacred Circle, one partner takes on the role of the speaker, embodying the masculine energy of expression and assertion. The other partner assumes the role of the listener, channelling the feminine energy of receptivity and understanding. The speaker shares their thoughts, feelings, or concerns openly, without interruption. This is a time for clear, direct communication, where the speaker has the floor to express what's on their mind and in their heart.

The listener, in turn, provides a safe, non-judgmental space for the speaker. They listen attentively, not interrupting or offering solutions unless asked. The act of listening is not passive; it's an active, empathetic engagement with the speaker, validating their feelings through attentive silence or non-verbal cues like nodding.

After a set period, or once the speaker feels they have fully expressed themselves, the roles switch. The listener becomes the speaker, and the speaker becomes the listener. This alternation allows both partners to experience the energies of both expression and reception, promoting a balanced dynamic within the relationship.

The Sacred Circle ritual can be as formal or as informal as you like. Some couples choose to create a special environment for it, lighting candles, playing soft music, or even creating a physical circle with stones or other natural elements. Others find that
 a simple, quiet space works best for them. The key is to make it a regular practice, whether weekly, bi-weekly, or monthly, to ensure that both partners have the opportunity to express and be heard, to lead and to follow.

By incorporating the Sacred Circle into your relationship rituals, you not only create a dedicated space for open communication but also actively engage in balancing the masculine and feminine energies within your relationship. It serves as a potent reminder that both speaking and listening, asserting and receiving, are essential for a harmonious, balanced partnership.

To truly embrace the dance of energies is to recognise the dynamic, ever-changing nature of relationships.

It's about understanding that in any given moment, one partner may resonate more with their masculine energy, and the other with their feminine, and then, without warning, the roles might reverse.

The ancients understood this fluidity, this impermanence, and they revered it. For us modern couples, this ancient wisdom serves as a guiding light, leading them towards a relationship that is balanced, harmonious, and deeply connected.

In my years of working with couples, I've observed that one of the most overlooked yet critical aspects of a fulfilling and enduring relationship is the balance of these energies. Often, couples are unaware of these underlying forces, leading to imbalances that manifest in various ways—be it emotional disconnect or conflict. The repercussions of such imbalances can be significant, and if not addressed lead to toxicity and even divorce. The good news is that the solution can be surprisingly simple, a little conscious effort and understanding can harmonise these energies and elevate a couple's relationship to great heights. For example James and Rebecca, and Sophia and Alex—illustrate how bringing awareness to this elemental aspect of relationships can lead to transformative changes. These couples were able to identify their dominant energies and take actionable steps to achieve a more balanced, fulfilling relationship. Their experiences serve as real-world examples that demonstrate the profound impact of achieving this sacred balance.

For example James and Rebecca. James, a corporate executive, was deeply entrenched in his Divine Masculine energy, which manifested in his focus on leadership, logic, action, and problem-solving. This made him highly effective in his professional life but left him feeling disconnected and frustrated at home. He found domestic life chaotic and was unsure how to engage meaningfully with his family, which led him to prioritise his career, a realm where he felt competent and understood his impact.

Rebecca, on the other hand, was a counsellor who naturally operated from her Divine Feminine energy, emphasising emotions, nurturing, and support. While this made her excellent at her job, it also left her emotionally drained. She felt overwhelmed trying to balance her professional responsibilities with taking care of their home life, including managing the children and household tasks. Rebecca found herself emotionally spent, constantly supporting everyone else but struggling with setting clear boundaries for her own well-being.

The imbalance in their energies was causing strain in their relationship and family dynamics. Rebecca felt like she was carrying the emotional and domestic burden alone, while James felt disconnected, unsure of how to contribute meaningfully to their home life.

Through some open honest conversation and conscious actions they were able to work together to embrace the opposite energy and balance their relationship. James started cooking, a task traditionally managed by Rebecca. This not only gave Rebecca some much-needed respite but also allowed James to connect with his family in a new, emotionally fulfilling way. James also started practising mindfulness and meditation. He initiated more conversations about feelings, hopes, and fears with Rebecca, and became more involved with their children, not just as a provider but as an emotionally available parent. As a result James also noticed a difference in his performance and that of his team at work.

Rebecca began to engage more in decision-making processes that she had previously left to James. She started setting boundaries at work and at home, allowing herself the space to focus on her own well-being. By consciously working to balance their Divine Feminine and Masculine energies, both James and Rebecca found that their relationship deepened and became more emotionally fulfilling. Rebecca felt supported and less overwhelmed, while James felt more connected and engaged in their family life. The act of achieving this balance enriched not only their relationship but their individual lives, making both of them more complete, well-rounded human beings.

While James and Rebecca's case illustrated the challenges that can arise when partners operate from opposite ends of the Divine Feminine and Masculine spectrum, problems can also manifest when couples find themselves too aligned in the same energy. This was the case for, Sophia and Alex, both artists by profession, who found themselves in a unique quandary. Their energies were strikingly similar, both operating predominantly from their Divine Feminine, which emphasised intuition, emotions, and creativity. While this similarity initially drew them together, providing a deep emotional and creative connection, it eventually led to a sense of stagnation in their relationship. They found themselves stuck in a loop of emotional intensity and creative exploration, without the grounding and direction that the Divine Masculine energy could provide. Their relationship began to feel like an endless brainstorming session with no execution.

For Sophia and Alex, we introduced new practices they could do together to balance their energies. They took up Tantra and couples' yoga, both ancient practices focusing on the union of Divine Feminine and Masculine energies. Tantra helped them connect on a deeper emotional and spiritual level, teaching them the art of giving and receiving, leading and following.

Couples' yoga, on the other hand, provided them with the grounding they needed, emphasising strength, focus, and balance, qualities often associated with the Divine Masculine. The impact of these practices was transformative. The newfound balance led to a more dynamic and fulfilling interaction. Conversations became more purposeful, emotional exchanges more grounded, and their creative collaborations took on a new life, enriched by the balanced energies they both brought to the table.

By consciously incorporating practices to balance their Divine Feminine and Masculine energies, Sophia and Alex not only revitalised their relationship but also found a new sense of purpose and direction in their individual lives. The stagnation was replaced by growth, the confusion by clarity, and the emotional intensity by a deep, grounded love.

The balance of Divine Feminine and Divine Masculine energies in a romantic relationship is a journey, not a destination. It requires constant effort, awareness, and the willingness to adapt and grow. However, the rewards are profound. A balanced relationship offers emotional depth, mutual growth, and a harmonious existence that enriches every aspect of life. By drawing on ancient wisdom and engaging in practical, modern solutions, couples can achieve this sacred balance, crafting a relationship that not only stands the test of time but also serves as a beacon of love, respect, and mutual fulfilment.

Chapter 6: The Art of Communication

In an age where emojis replace words and social media 'likes' are mistaken for meaningful connections, the art of genuine communication is becoming endangered. This is especially troubling for our romantic relationships, where the stakes are high and the repercussions of miscommunication can be devastating. While technology has given us more ways to connect it has also made it easier to avoid the deep, uncomfortable, and necessary conversations that sustain a relationship. The result? A growing chasm between partners is filled with misunderstandings, unmet expectations, and emotional disconnection.

Communication is the lifeblood of all human relationships. From the ancient tribes that gathered around roaring fires to the sprawling cities of Mesopotamia, the ability to convey thoughts, feelings, and ideas has always been central to our existence. The ancients understood this deeply, crafting intricate systems and methodologies for communication, not only in practical terms but also in the deeper, more intimate layers of human connection.

Before the written word became widespread, our ancestors depended on symbols and oral narratives to pass down knowledge, wisdom, and values. These symbols, whether etched on cave walls or woven into tapestries, were more than just depictions; they were the earliest forms of communication. They told stories of heroism, love, tragedy, and triumph.

Stories, especially held immense power. They were not merely tales, but tools for teaching lessons, conveying morals, and bonding communities. Through stories, ancient societies could navigate complex emotions, teach the younger generations about their heritage, and even discuss challenging topics which prepare them for deeper communication and connection in their intimate relationships.

The Power of Listening
Ancient cultures placed a significant emphasis on the act of listening. In ancient African cultures, the Griots, or storytellers, held a special place in society. They were revered not only for their ability to weave tales but also for their skill in listening. They were the keepers of oral tradition, absorbing the stories of the old and passing them on to the next generation. This art of listening was not just about hearing words but understanding their weight and significance.

Listening in many ancient societies was seen as a form of respect. It indicated a willingness to understand, to empathise, and to connect on a deeper level. Many indigenous cultures emphasised the importance of sitting in circles during community gatherings to ensure everyone had an equal opportunity to speak and be heard. This cultural listening made for stronger romantic relationships too.

Communication as a Sacred Act
In ancient Egyptian society, the concept of Ma'at represented truth, balance, and order. Communication, especially truthful communication, was seen as a sacred act that maintained the balance of Ma'at. Similarly, the ancient Indian scripture, the Rigveda, spoke of "Vak" or the divine speech, highlighting the spiritual significance of communication.

These ancient cultures understood that communication was more than just a transaction; it was an exchange of energy, a melding of souls. Words held power and they were to be used responsibly and with intention.

So, how can we apply this ancient wisdom to our modern relationships?

Mindful Speaking

Mindful speaking is more than just choosing the right words; it's about understanding the power those words have to shape reality, influence emotions, and define relationships. In a world where communication is often reduced to hastily typed texts and emojis, the art of mindful speaking has never been more critical. When you speak with intention and clarity, you're not just conveying information; you're inviting an authentic exchange, setting the stage for meaningful interaction and deeper understanding. Growing up you may have heard the saying sticks and stones may break my bones but words will never hurt me, now we know that is not true. Our words matter, what is said, how it is said as well as what is not said, and it is our relationships and emotional well-being that suffer the most when we get this wrong.

The ancients understood this well. Their oral traditions, philosophical dialogues, and even their epic tales were all exercises in mindful speaking and listening. They recognised that words could be vessels of wisdom, carriers of culture, and the glue that binds a community together.In relationships, the way we communicate with our partners can either nurture the connection or undermine it. It's important to recognise that sometimes we might unintentionally talk to our partners in a way that's not our best.

To practise mindful speaking, start by being fully present in the conversation. This means not just hearing, but actively listening to your partner. Before you speak, take a moment to consider the impact of your words. Are they constructive or destructive? Are they coming from a place of love, or from a place of ego? Are you seeking to understand, or are you merely waiting for your turn to speak?

Clarity is another crucial aspect of mindful speaking. In a relationship, misunderstandings can easily arise from vague or ambiguous statements. Being clear about what you mean minimises the chances of misinterpretation and allows a more open dialogue to take place.

Lastly, be aware of not just what you say, but how you say it. Tone, volume, and even the pace of your speech can all convey additional layers of meaning. A soft tone can turn a critique into constructive feedback, while a harsh tone can turn even a compliment into a point of contention.

In essence, mindful speaking is about respecting the power of words and using them wisely. It's about recognising that every word you speak is a choice and making those choices in a way that enriches, rather than depletes, your relationship.

Active Listening

In today's fast-paced, technology-driven world, the art of active listening has become increasingly rare, yet its importance in relationships is more crucial than ever. Active listening goes beyond the passive act of hearing; it's an engaged form of communication that involves understanding, empathising, and responding thoughtfully to your partner. It's not just about the words being spoken, but also the emotions and intentions behind them.

To truly listen, you must first be present in the moment. This means setting aside all distractions, both physical and mental. Put down your phone, turn off the TV, and give your partner your undivided attention. Afterall what is more important and deserves your attention more than the person you love? Being present also means quieting your own internal dialogue. It's easy to start formulating a response while your partner is still speaking, but doing so means you're not fully engaged in listening. Instead, focus on what's being said, how it's being said, and even what's not being said—sometimes, non-verbal cues can speak volumes.

Being present allows you to better understand your partner's perspective, validating their feelings and making them feel heard and respected. This, in turn, creates a deeper emotional connection, creating a virtuous cycle that strengthens your bond. It's a level of intimacy that goes beyond the physical, touching the very core of your relationship.

Active listening also involves empathising with your partner. This doesn't mean you have to agree with everything they say, but rather that you try to understand things from their point of view. Empathy can defuse tension, resolve conflicts, and bring you closer as a couple.

Finally, active listening involves thoughtful responses. This means not just reacting impulsively, but taking the time to consider what's been said and then responding in a way that adds constructively to the conversation. Whether it's offering support, asking for clarification, or sharing your own perspective, your response should aim to deepen the connection and mutual understanding between you and your partner.

Making the conscious effort to actively listen can set the stage for a deeper, more meaningful relationship. It's a simple yet powerful way to strengthen your bond and enrich your emotional connection.

Non-verbal Communication
Given that 93% of communication is non-verbal I cannot emphasise its importance, especially in our romantic relationships, where understanding and intimacy are key. If your partner's love language is

physical touch, mastering the art of non-verbal communication becomes not just important, but a double win, enhancing the emotional and physical bond between you. Pay attention to body language, tone, and other non-verbal cues. Ancient cultures used dance, art, and rituals to express themselves; we can do the same today. Get imaginative with your partner - dance, do creative projects together to express yourself.

Understanding Love Languages
One of the best discoveries in relationship psychology in recent times is the "Five Love Languages," developed by Dr. Gary Chapman. This concept has been nothing short of revolutionary for modern relationships and is something I recommend to all my clients having experienced the benefits first hand in my own marriage. This framework identifies the primary ways people feel loved and appreciated: words of affirmation, physical touch, acts of service, quality time, and receiving gifts. Understanding these love languages isn't just a trendy relationship tip, it's a powerful tool for deepening emotional connections and enhancing mutual understanding in a relationship.

When you know your partner's primary love language, you gain invaluable insight into what makes them feel truly loved and valued. For instance, if your partner's love language is words of affirmation, simple phrases like "I love you," "You're amazing," or "I'm proud of you" can have a profound impact on their emotional well-being. On the other hand, if their love language is acts of service, actions like making them a cup of tea or taking care of a chore they dislike can speak volumes. But the benefits don't stop at just knowing each other's love languages, it's about applying this knowledge consistently in your daily life. It's one thing to know that your partner values quality time, but it's another to actively carve out special moments together, free from distractions. Similarly, if physical touch is important to your partner, then regular hugs, kisses, and cuddles become not just physical interactions, but deeply emotional ones.

Understanding love languages can also be a game-changer during conflicts or stressful times. When tensions are high it's easy to forget how to effectively communicate love and appreciation, but if you know that your partner responds well to, for example, acts of service, doing something helpful can ease tension and open the door for more effective communication.

It's also worth noting that people can have secondary love languages or appreciate a combination of them. The key is to not just understand these languages intellectually but to put them into practice. It's an ongoing process that requires attention, effort, and a genuine desire to make your partner feel loved.

In a world where relationships can be complicated by numerous external factors, the concept of love languages simplifies the complexities of emotional connections. It offers a straightforward yet deeply effective roadmap for long-lasting, fulfilling relationships. By consistently speaking your partner's love language, you're not just saying you love them, you're showing it in the way that resonates with them the most. And that can make all the difference.

The Power of Storytelling
The art of storytelling is as ancient as human civilisation itself, serving as a linch pin for community building, education, and emotional connection. Sharing personal experiences or complex ideas through stories isn't just a way to convey information; it's a method for deepening emotional bonds and creating a shared narrative.

When you share a personal experience as a story you're doing more than just recounting events. You're inviting your partner into your world, offering them a glimpse into your thoughts, feelings, and emotions. You're saying, "This is a part of me, and I want to share it with you." This act of vulnerability can be incredibly powerful, creating a deeper emotional connection and a stronger sense of intimacy.

Moreover, storytelling allows for the richness and complexity of experiences to be fully appreciated. It provides context, evokes emotions, and invites engagement. When you share a story, you're not just talking to your partner; you're creating an interactive experience that invites questions, insights, and a deeper understanding of each other's lives and perspectives.

In a world where many people feel increasingly isolated—despite being more "connected" than ever, storytelling serves as a potent antidote to loneliness and emotional detachment. It can be a way to build not just romantic relationships but also community bonds. Whether it's sharing stories around a dinner table, recounting fond memories, or even discussing challenges, the act of storytelling creates a sense of belonging and togetherness.

But storytelling isn't just about speaking; it's also about listening. When your partner shares a story with you giving them your full attention shows that you value their experiences and perspectives. This reciprocal act of sharing and listening can create a virtuous cycle of empathy and understanding in your relationship.

In essence, storytelling is a multi-dimensional form of communication that engages the emotional, intellectual, and even spiritual aspects of our being. It's a way to transcend the superficialities of everyday conversation and tap into something much deeper and more meaningful. By incorporating storytelling into your relationship, you're not just sharing words; you're building a shared narrative, enriching your emotional connection, and, in the process, strengthening the very fabric of your relationship.

Chapter 7: Achieving Harmony through Conflict Resolution

Conflict is inevitable in every healthy relationship. A common misconception is that the opposite of love is hate. In my experience the opposite of love is indifference. When a couple is arguing or in conflict, it is usually a sign there are feelings between them and there is a chance of improving the relationship as opposed to those who come to see me who have already checked out and there is no going back. It's not the presence of conflict but how we handle it that truly matters. We all have triggers—those sensitive areas that can easily set us off into emotional turmoil. Knowing your own triggers, as well as your partner's, can be a game-changer in how you navigate disagreements.

Seek the good intention
Look for understanding over being right in an argument. This approach not only diffuses conflicts but also deepens the emotional connection between you and your partner. Instead of focusing on the heat of the moment or the clumsy execution of words, aim to find the positive intention behind your partner's actions or statements. Assume that their intentions

are good, even if their actions or words trigger you. Give them the opportunity to try again, you might say something like, "I'm sure you didn't mean to upset me, but what I heard was [insert trigger]. I know that's probably not what you intended. Could you please clarify?"

If the emotional atmosphere becomes too charged, consider taking a step back to gain perspective. If possible, spend some time in nature. The tranquillity of the natural world helps to calm heightened emotions through the release of feel-good hormones endorphins, dopamine, serotonin and oxytocin which allows you to think clearer.

Take Responsibility
Taking responsibility for your relationship and your behaviour is crucial for a thriving partnership. It's easy to point fingers, to lay blame on your partner when things go awry, but true growth and connection come from looking inward first. This isn't about shouldering all the blame or becoming a martyr for the relationship; it's about acknowledging your role in the dynamics between you and your partner.
When you take responsibility, you empower yourself and, by extension, your relationship. You become an active participant in your relationship capable of enacting change and nurturing a deeper connection. It means owning your mistakes and learning from

them, but also celebrating your contributions to the love and joy in your partnership.

This act of taking responsibility is a two-way street. It involves open communication where both partners can express how they feel their needs are being met, and where they think they could improve. It's a continual process of checking in, reassessing, and realigning yourselves with each other and the relationship's goals.

By taking responsibility, you're not just fixing problems; you're elevating your relationship to a level of conscious coupling, where both partners are fully engaged in nurturing a fulfilling, respectful, and loving environment. It's a commitment to a shared life that isn't just good, but extraordinary.

The Art of Apologising and Forgiveness
A relationship is not able to be extraordinary unless you both learn the art of apologising and forgiveness and commit to doing it. Accepting that there will be moments in your relationships where you will both need to be able to apologise and forgive each other and yourselves is key. They are the mechanisms that repair tears, mend frays, and strengthen weak spots. Without them, even the most loving relationship can unravel over time.

Forgiveness is not just a one-time act but a continuous process, a conscious decision to release feelings of resentment or vengeance toward someone who has harmed you regardless of whether they actually deserve your forgiveness. It's a gift you give to yourself as much as to your partner. Holding onto grudges and past hurts not only poisons your relationship but also your own well-being. Forgiveness doesn't mean forgetting or excusing the harm done to you, it means liberating yourself from the burden of ongoing bitterness and making room for peace, hope, and even reconciliation. It's fundamental for emotional freedom and a prerequisite for the growth and depth of any relationship.

An apology is not just saying "I'm sorry." It's acknowledging your mistake, understanding the pain you've caused and committing to making amends. A genuine apology is a powerful tool that can heal emotional wounds, dissolve anger and bitterness, and restore trust. The art of apologising involves several key steps: acknowledging the wrong done, expressing regret and seeking a way to make amends. It's not about offering excuses or justifications. It is about taking responsibility for your actions and showing that you're committed to change.

Forgiveness and apology are two sides of the same coin; they work best in tandem. An apology opens the door for forgiveness, and forgiveness confirms the sincerity of an apology. Together, they create a virtuous cycle that reinforces emotional bonds and deepens trust.

Take, for example, Ethan and Olivia. Both are career-oriented individuals, juggling the demands of their jobs with the responsibilities of raising their children. While they love each other deeply, their contrasting backgrounds and communication styles led to a series of misunderstandings and resentments that have begun to strain their relationship.

Ethan grew up in a household where conflicts were resolved through loud, passionate arguments. For him, shouting was a form of engagement, a way to hash things out until a resolution was reached. Olivia, on the other hand, was raised in an environment where conflicts were swept under the rug, where the prevailing ethos was to avoid confrontation at all costs. This led to a dynamic where Ethan perceived Olivia's avoidance as dismissive and hurtful while Olivia felt that Ethan's shouting was aggressive and overwhelming. Ethan also had difficulty articulating apologies. He believed he expressed regret through his actions or indirect words, but Olivia didn't hear it because he hadn't used the specific phrase "I'm sorry," which to her signifies a genuine acknowledgement of wrongdoing. This led Olivia to harbour lingering resentments, feeling that her emotions and experiences were not being validated.

Recognising that their relationship was at a critical juncture, Ethan and Olivia committed to open communication to understand each other's perspectives better. They agreed that when conflicts arose, they would first try to understand the other's good intentions before reacting. Ethan learnt to temper his confrontational style, taking a step back to allow both of them the space to cool off before revisiting the issue. Olivia, in turn, committed to facing issues head-on, learning to articulate her feelings calmly rather than avoiding confrontation.

Through this new approach, Ethan finally understood the power of a heartfelt "I'm sorry," and Olivia learned to appreciate that Ethan's loud expressions were not attacks but rather a different form of engagement. Both committed to ongoing dialogue and self-reflection, realising that the key to resolving their conflicts lay not just in the words they used, but in understanding the emotional and historical contexts that shaped their communication styles.

By taking responsibility for their actions and committing to change, Ethan and Olivia were able to transform their relationship. They learned the art of apologising and forgiving, not just as reactive measures, but as proactive strategies to deepen their emotional connection, build trust, and create a loving, resilient relationship. Through this conscious effort, they didn't just patch up their relationship; they fortified it, creating a stronger, more harmonious union.

In order to apologise and forgive wholeheartedly you need to go through the following steps:

- **Open Dialogue:** The first step in either forgiveness or apology is open, honest communication. Discuss the issue without blame or judgement, focusing on feelings and impacts.
- **Self-Reflection:** Before you can genuinely forgive or apologise, you need to understand your own feelings and motivations. Take some time to reflect on what led to the situation and how it affected both parties.
- **Express and Accept:** If you're apologising, clearly express your regret and outline how you plan to make amends. If you're forgiving, explicitly state that you forgive your partner and are willing to move forward.
- **Commit to Change:** Both forgiveness and apology involve a commitment to change. Whether it's promising never to commit the same mistake or agreeing to let go of resentment, this commitment is crucial for the relationship to move forward.
- **Reaffirm Your Love:** After the process of forgiveness or apology, it's essential to reaffirm

your love and commitment to each other. This helps to reset the emotional tone of the relationship and start anew.

Forgiveness and apology are not just reactive measures to deal with conflict; they're proactive strategies to deepen your emotional connection, build trust, and create a loving, resilient relationship

Be the hero
Another approach is to "race to be the hero" in the relationship. This means striving to be the first to apologise or resolve the conflict. It's a shift in mindset from seeking to be right to seeking understanding and harmony. When both partners adopt this attitude, it creates a nurturing environment where you both feel valued and heard.

While the mediums have changed, the essence of communication remains the same. It's about respect, intention, and genuine connection. By applying these timeless principles, we can bridge the emotional gaps that have crept into our relationships. We can rekindle the ancient flame of genuine communication, ensuring that our modern relationships are as emotionally rich and fulfilling as they were meant to be.

Get to know your triggers

Understanding we all have triggers is the first step in transforming how we handle conflict in our relationships. Triggers are those emotional hot buttons that, when pushed, can lead to disproportionate reactions and escalate conflicts. Knowing what these triggers are for both you and your partner is transformative because it allows you to navigate conflicts with greater awareness and sensitivity. But awareness alone isn't enough; the next step is to work on mitigating these triggers. Sometimes this involves getting to the root cause of why certain words or actions provoke such strong reactions. This can be a deep and sometimes challenging process that may benefit from the guidance of a professional, such as a relationship coach or therapist. An objective third party can provide valuable insights into the dynamics at play and offer strategies for de-escalation and constructive communication.

Show Compassion
In the journey of love and partnership showing compassion stands as one of the most transformative acts you can engage in. It's more than just a fleeting emotion, it's a stance, a way of being that enriches both you and your partner. Compassion invites you to see the good intent in your partner, even when their actions might suggest otherwise. It's the lens that allows you to view conflicts as opportunities for deeper understanding rather than as threats to your

relationship. But compassion isn't just outward; it's also about extending that same grace to yourself. In the complexities of modern life and relationships, it's easy to be your own harshest critic. By showing compassion to yourself, you're not just improving your own well-being, but also bringing a healthier, more empathetic self into the relationship.

Lean in and learn
Leaning into conflict rather than shying away from it offers a valuable opportunity for growth, both individually and as a couple. Conflict is often seen as something to be avoided, but when approached constructively it can actually strengthen your relationship and build resilience. Learning from conflict means not just resolving the issue at hand, but also gaining insights into your own behaviour and that of your partner. It's about making conscious decisions on how to handle similar situations in the future.

For instance, both my husband and I have recognised that we need to step away and get some space when triggered. For me, that sanctuary is often found in nature. Taking the dog for a walk allows me to clear my head, breathe, and approach the situation with a calmer demeanour. My husband, on the other hand, finds his emotional equilibrium through physical activity, like chopping wood for example, which allows him to release any pent-up frustration. The key is that

we don't sweep the issue under the rug; we are committed to addressing the "elephant in the room," but only when we're both emotionally ready to do so. This conscious approach to timing has a dual benefit. First, it prevents conflicts from escalating into more damaging territory where things might be said that are later regretted. Second,
 it provides an opportunity for introspection, allowing us to consider how our own behaviour affects our partner. This is crucial for mutual understanding and growth.

By leaning into conflict and learning from it you are not just putting out fires you're fireproofing your relationship. You're building resilience by equipping yourselves with the tools and strategies to handle future conflicts which are inevitable in any long-term relationship. This resilience doesn't just make your relationship stronger it also enriches your emotional life, providing a sense of security and mutual respect that can weather any storm.

Chapter 8: Sensuality and Intimacy

In today's hyper-connected yet emotionally distant world, the decline in genuine intimacy and communication is reaching alarming levels. Recent studies indicate that nearly 20% of married couples have sex fewer than 10 times a year, revealing a crisis of physical intimacy. Even more concerning sexless marriages are becoming increasingly common and research suggests that the lack of physical intimacy in these unions can lead to infidelity. Estimates indicate that about 20-40% of married individuals engage in extramarital affairs at some point.

This absence of closeness doesn't merely affect the bedroom it reverberates through every aspect of a relationship. It leads to emotional disconnection, feelings of neglect, and loneliness. The repercussions are severe, affecting not just the emotional, but also the psychological well-being of individuals. The human touch, which releases oxytocin—the "love hormone"—becomes rare, leading to increased stress, anxiety and depression. This hormone is crucial for nurturing feelings of bonding and security and its absence can lead to low self-esteem and a sense of unworthiness.

Moreover, the neglect of physical intimacy can give rise to resentment, frustration, and a sense of unmet needs. This emotional void can sometimes even lead individuals to seek fulfilment outside the relationship causing a breakdown in trust and further exacerbating the issue. The problem becomes even more complex when there's a lack of emotional connection which serves as the foundation for a healthy and satisfying sexual relationship. Without emotional intimacy couples may struggle to express their true selves and experience genuine closeness, leading to detachment, dissatisfaction, and strain within the relationship.

As a relationship coach who has worked extensively with couples on the brink of separation and those who have already made the painful decision to divorce, I can attest that infidelity is often a symptom of a deeper issue. It's the canary in the coal mine signalling a lack of both physical and emotional intimacy. The repercussions of this absence are severe affecting not just the emotional, but also the psychological well-being of both partners. The human touch, a simple act that releases oxytocin—often referred to as the "love hormone"—becomes a rare commodity. This leads to increased stress, anxiety, and depression, further widening the emotional chasm between partners.

In the case of Emily and Mark, both successful professionals, who seemed to have it all. They were deeply in love, they had a disposable income, travelled together, and had a fulfilling sex life. However, things took a turn when they started a family. Emily's career took a back seat as she focused on their new baby finding her needs for love and connection met through motherhood and her new social circle of other mums.

Mark, on the other hand, felt a void where he once found connection and significance with Emily. He began to invest more in his work where he felt appreciated and rewarded. His career soared to new heights, but it demanded more of his time and attention often requiring him to travel.

Over time and with the birth of their second child the distance between them grew both emotionally and physically. They stopped being intimate, not just because Mark was often away, but also because Emily was exhausted from taking care of the kids and had lost confidence in her post-pregnancy body. Things drifted to a point where Mark, feeling emotionally disconnected at home, had an affair. Emily was blindsided; she never saw it coming.
The demands of family life, coupled with the shifting dynamics in their relationship, had created a perfect storm. What was once an exciting, fulfilling partnership had taken a back seat to their new roles as parents and professionals. They had lost their way with devastating consequences. Unfortunately for Emily

and Mark, the damage was too great to repair and the couple divorced.

This story is far from unique; it's a narrative that plays out in countless relationships. The drift begins subtly but can lead to a chasm so wide that couples find it almost impossible to bridge. It's a cautionary tale that underscores the importance of maintaining both emotional and physical intimacy in a relationship especially when navigating the complexities of family life and career demands.

What can we glean from how ancient cultures nurtured intimacy and communication to rekindle and deepen our connections today and avoid the trappings of unfulfilled relationships?

Throughout history sensuality and intimacy have been integral to the human experience. The city of Pompeii, frozen in time by volcanic ash, reveals lovers caught in their final moments in a deep embrace. This poignant scene serves as a timeless testament to the enduring nature of love.

In ancient India the Kama Sutra wasn't merely a manual for intimate positions, but a comprehensive guide to the art of living, emphasising the importance of emotional connection and desire. Ancient Chinese couples performed the "three bows" to symbolise their union, while African tribes practised the art of "sitting in the moonlight," discussing dreams and fears under the stars. These rituals and practices underscored the multi-dimensional nature of intimacy incorporating emotional, spiritual and physical elements.

Many ancient societies viewed intimacy as a sacred act. In ancient Egypt, the goddess Hathor was invoked for blessings, as intimacy was considered a way to honour the divine. Tantric practices from ancient India focused on the merging of souls and the exchange of energies, allowing couples to reach profound emotional and spiritual depths.

Ancient cultures placed significant emphasis on emotional depth and the art of listening. The Griots in ancient African cultures were revered for their storytelling and their ability to listen, absorb and pass on stories from one generation to the next. In ancient Egyptian society, the concept of Ma'at represented truth, balance and order making communication a sacred act that maintained this balance.

Today, the challenge is how to cultivate intimacy in a world that often feels too busy for genuine connection. When it comes to intimacy and relationships, men and women often seek different paths to fulfilment though the end goal of a deep meaningful connection is the same. For many men, physical intimacy is a crucial way to express love and affection. It's not solely about the sexual act but also the emotional closeness, affirmation, and acceptance that come with it. Men often look for validation in intimacy, where feeling desired or needed can significantly boost their self-esteem. In most cultures' where societal norms encourage men to suppress their emotions, intimacy with a partner provides a 'safe space' for them to be vulnerable and express their feelings without judgement.

On the other hand, women frequently view emotional intimacy as the base upon which physical intimacy can be genuinely fulfilling. The act of sharing, listening and emotionally connecting can significantly enhance the sexual experience for many women. Without this emotional foundation, the physical act can feel hollow. Security and trust are also paramount; women often need to feel emotionally supported to fully engage in and enjoy physical intimacy. This sense of security is nurtured through consistent emotional support, open communication, and acts that affirm commitment. Additionally, women often appreciate the nuances of the intimate experience more than the end goal. Attention to detail like setting the mood, engaging in

foreplay and providing aftercare can profoundly impact a woman's overall experience.
Understanding these general tendencies can offer valuable insights into creating a fulfilling intimate relationship for both partners. It's essential to remember that these are not strict rules, but general observations, and the most crucial factor is open communication between partners to understand each other's unique needs and desires.

With that in mind, how do you create a fulfilling intimate relationship with your partner? These are some of the key things to consider.

Meeting each other's needs
A fundamental element of a fulfilling relationship is understanding and meeting each other's basic human needs. These needs are primal, deeply ingrained in our psyche, and drive our behaviour in profound ways. Meeting these needs is not just crucial for our happiness, but also for the success and longevity of our relationships. As a relationship coach, I've seen the transformative power of understanding and meeting these needs in a relationship. My husband and I practise a monthly "needs check-in," a strategy I also recommend to my clients, with a high rate of success.

What are the six human needs?

Certainty

Certainty is the need for safety, stability, and comfort in our lives. It can be met through open and honest communication, consistent acts of love and kindness, and financial planning as a couple. However, it can also be met in unhealthy ways, such as through over-controlling behaviour or emotional manipulation.

Variety
Variety is the need for change, challenges, and excitement. Healthy ways to meet this need include trying new activities together, surprising each other, and keeping an element of mystery in the relationship. Unhealthy ways include engaging in risky behaviours or having emotional or physical affairs.

Significance
Significance is the need to feel unique, important, and valued. This need can be met through regularly expressing appreciation for each other, celebrating each other's achievements and listening actively and attentively. Unhealthy ways to meet this need include putting down your partner to elevate yourself or seeking validation from external sources like social media or work.

Love & Connection
Love and connection is the need to feel connected with, and loved by other human beings. This need can be met through quality time together, physical intimacy, and emotional vulnerability. However, it can

also be met in unhealthy ways, such as through emotional dependency or manipulating emotions to gain affection.

Growth
Growth is the law of the universe if something is not growing it is dying, and nothing is not moving. In us humans it is the need for emotional, intellectual, and spiritual development. This need can be met through learning together, setting and achieving goals as a couple, and encouraging each other's individual pursuits. Unhealthy ways to meet this need include becoming overly competitive with each other or suppressing each other's growth for fear of growing apart.

Evolution
Evolution has shown us that anything that is not contributing to the environment and development of the world is removed. Contribution is the need to give beyond ourselves and make a difference. This need can be met through volunteering together, supporting each other's individual efforts to contribute to society and acts of kindness towards each other and others. Unhealthy ways to meet this need include sacrificing your own needs consistently to meet your partner's or losing your sense of self in the act of giving.

A healthy practice to get into is to regularly check in with your partner on how you are meeting your own and each other's needs. My husband and I do this every month which is a practice I have seen work wonders with clients. During this time we rate on a scale of 1-10 how well each of these six basic human needs is being met in our relationship and in our individual lives. A score of 10 means the need is fully met. We then discuss these scores, identify any gaps, and strategise on how we can support each other in meeting these needs more effectively. This practice has been incredibly enlightening and has helped us navigate the complexities of a long-term relationship with greater ease.

Understanding and meeting each other's basic human needs is not just a strategy for relationship success; it's a blueprint for individual happiness. When these needs are not met within the relationship we will inevitably seek to fulfil them elsewhere often in ways that can be detrimental to the relationship. By regularly checking in with each other through practices like our monthly "needs check-in," you not only keep the lines of communication open, but also deepen your understanding of yourselves and each other. This paves the way for a more fulfilling, harmonious relationship.

Sacred Spaces

Creating a sacred space for intimacy doesn't require a lavish setup or a room straight out of "Fifty Shades of Grey" unless, of course, that's your preference and you have the means to make it happen. The key is to establish areas in your home that are sanctuaries for emotional and physical connection, free from the distractions that modern life so often throws our way.

In today's world, technology is a constant presence, and it's all too easy to let it invade every corner of our lives including our most intimate moments. That's why it's crucial to set boundaries. The bedroom, for example, should be a haven for sleep and intimacy. When you bring in distractions like TV or smartphones you dilute the room's primary purpose. By keeping these devices out you're sending a clear message: this space is for us, for our connection and for our well-being.

Creating a tech-free zone doesn't have to be complicated. It can be as simple as deciding that the bedroom is a phone-free area after a certain hour or investing in some soft lighting and comfortable pillows to make the space more inviting. You might also consider adding elements that engage the senses, like scented candles or soft music, to make the environment more conducive to intimacy.

The point is to create a physical space that reflects the emotional and spiritual connection you seek. When you step into this space, you should feel as though you're stepping away from the chaos of daily life and into a sanctuary where your relationship is the focus. This simple act of designating a 'sacred space' can have a profound impact on the quality of your connection with your partner.

Scheduled Intimacy
The concept of scheduling intimacy may sound counterintuitive, but it's a practical and effective solution to a modern problem. Our lives are filled with endless tasks, responsibilities, and distractions. Between work, childcare, social obligations, and the constant pings from our devices, finding spontaneous moments for intimacy can be difficult and banking on you both having the energy at the end of the day is not a great strategy particularly if you both take your phones to bed.

By setting aside a specific time each week for intimacy, you're not only making a commitment to your partner but also to the health and longevity of your relationship. This act of scheduling becomes a modern ritual, a sacred space in your week that is free from distractions and interruptions. It's a time when both partners can focus solely on each other, to explore, connect, and deepen their emotional and physical bond.

Moreover, knowing that you have this time set aside can build anticipation and excitement, enhancing the overall experience. It creates a psychological space where both partners can prepare mentally and emotionally, making the time spent together more meaningful and fulfilling.

So, while it may seem strange at first, scheduling intimacy is a practical way to ensure that you're making time for each other in a world that constantly pulls us in different directions. It's a commitment to maintaining the emotional and physical closeness that is so crucial for a healthy thriving relationship. And in a way it's a nod to the wisdom of our ancestors who understood the importance of dedicating time and space to celebrate love and intimacy.

The Power of Touch
The power of touch is so potent that it can convey a range of emotions—from love and comfort to empathy and support—often more accurately than words can. A hug, a gentle squeeze of the hand, or even a pat on the back can speak volumes, offering a sense of closeness and comfort that words sometimes fail to capture.

This is particularly true for those whose primary love language is physical touch. For these individuals, physical touch is not just a way to feel close; it's their primary mode of connecting emotionally with their partner. If your partner's love language is physical touch, understanding this can be a game-changer in your relationship. It means that even the smallest gestures—a kiss goodbye in the morning, a cuddle on the couch, or a simple touch on the arm—can have a profound impact on their emotional well-being.

But the importance of touch extends beyond those who identify it as their primary love language. Various studies have shown that touch releases oxytocin, often referred to as the "love hormone," which plays a crucial role in bonding and increases feelings of social bonding, emotional support, and relationship satisfaction. This biochemical reaction is a testament to how deeply ingrained the need for touch is in our human makeup.

Incorporating more touch into your relationship doesn't have to be complicated or overly orchestrated. It can be as simple as holding hands while you walk, offering a foot massage after a long day, or cuddling while you watch a movie. These acts, simple though they may be, serve to deepen your emotional connection, enhance your sense of intimacy, and strengthen your relationship. By consciously incorporating more tactile expressions of love into your relationship, you're not just improving your emotional bond—you're speaking a universal language that has been understood and cherished for millennia.

Emotional Vulnerability

Intimacy is often misunderstood as solely a sexual or physical experience. While those aspects are undeniably important, intimacy is a multifaceted concept that goes far beyond the physicality. One of the most crucial, yet often overlooked, facets is emotional intimacy, which serves as the bedrock upon which a fulfilling relationship is built.

Ancient cultures were keenly aware of the power of emotional connection. The stories that have survived through millennia, from the tragic love of Orpheus and Eurydice in Greek mythology to the passionate romance of Layla and Majnun in Persian literature, all emphasise the depth of emotional intimacy. These tales often explore the vulnerabilities, fears, dreams, and desires of their characters, revealing that the emotional bonds formed were just as significant—if not more so—than any physical connection.

Sharing fears, dreams, and desires isn't just about getting things off your chest; it's about allowing your partner into the most private corners of your heart and mind. This level of vulnerability can be intimidating but is essential for deepening your emotional bond. When you share your innermost thoughts and feelings, you're essentially saying, "I trust you with the real me, not just the version of me that the world sees."

This emotional vulnerability is not a one-time event but an ongoing process. Just as ancient stories were told and retold to impart wisdom and share experiences, couples need to continually share their evolving fears, dreams and desires to maintain a deep emotional connection.

Rediscovering the Senses
We often reduce intimacy to its physical or emotional components, forgetting that it's a multi-dimensional experience that can engage all our senses. By consciously incorporating sight, sound, smell, taste, and touch into your intimate moments, you can elevate the experience to a whole new level, making it more fulfilling and memorable for both you and your partner.

Consider all your senses
Sight
The visual aspect of intimacy is often underestimated. The ambience of the room, the lighting, and even the attire can significantly impact the mood. Soft, warm lighting can create a cosy, inviting atmosphere, while candles or fairy lights can add a touch of romance. The visual cues you offer each other—eye contact, facial

expressions, body language—can also deepen your connection.

Sound

Sound plays a crucial role in setting the mood. Whether it's the soft strumming of a guitar, the sensual notes of a jazz saxophone, or even the natural sounds of waves crashing or rain falling, the right auditory environment can make the experience more immersive. Your voices, too, are part of this soundscape—soft whispers, laughter, and verbal affirmations can enhance your emotional connection.

Smell

Aromas have a powerful impact on our emotions and can instantly transport us to different states of mind. Using aromatic oils or incense can not only make the environment more pleasant but also trigger positive emotional responses. Scents like lavender can calm the mind, while sandalwood or ylang-ylang can evoke a more sensual atmosphere.

Taste

Sharing a meal or even just some chocolate and wine can be an intimate experience. Feeding each other can be both playful and nurturing, adding another layer to your emotional bond. Foods like strawberries, chocolate, and oysters are often considered aphrodisiacs and incorporating them into your intimate moments can add a fun, experimental element.

Touch

Touch is perhaps the most obvious but also the most versatile of the senses when it comes to intimacy. It's not just about the sexual touch but also about the comforting hug, the playful tickle, or the reassuring hand on the shoulder. Different kinds of touch can convey different emotions—love, desire, comfort, reassurance—and understanding this language can make your relationship more nuanced and satisfying.

By consciously engaging all your senses, you can create a more holistic, enriching experience of intimacy. It's like listening to a symphony instead of a solo instrument; the richness lies in the harmony of the different elements coming together. So the next time you're looking to deepen your intimate connection, remember to engage all your senses. It's not just about feeling good; it's about feeling more, in every sense of the word.

Chapter 9: Raising Children with Ancient Wisdom

Every civilisation, from the tranquil valleys of ancient China to the rugged terrains of Greece, has grappled with the profound responsibility of raising the next generation. These societies have embedded their collective wisdom, values, and hopes into their young ones, creating a legacy that transcends time. As modern parents, we have the opportunity to use these ancient lessons into our own parenting approaches, emphasising not just academic or material success, but also compassion, courage, and the delicate balance between masculine and feminine energies.

The saying "it takes a village to raise a child" is more than just a proverb; it's a philosophy that has been lived out in various cultures throughout history. In ancient African societies, for example, children were considered a communal responsibility. Every member of the community, from the elders to the artisans, had a role in nurturing their growth. This collective approach ensured that children received diverse forms of love, guidance, and discipline, enriching their emotional and intellectual development.

In today's fragmented societies, where families are often dispersed and individualism is prized, recreating this "village" can be a challenge. However, the core principle remains invaluable. By surrounding our children with a network of caregivers—be it extended family members, mentors, teachers, or community leaders—we expose them to a spectrum of wisdom, values, and life skills. This multi-faceted support system can help children navigate the complexities of modern life, from social dynamics to emotional well-being.

The absence of this "village" in modern society has given rise to a host of issues. Loneliness, for instance, is increasingly reported among children and adolescents. The rise of social media has also correlated with a significant increase in rates of anxiety, depression, and even suicide among young people. According to recent studies, there has been a 56% rise in suicide among young girls since the advent of social media. The erosion of close-knit communities exposes children to potential dangers and mental health issues, making the need for a supportive "village" even more crucial.

In ancient Sparta, courage and resilience were mainstays of upbringing. While the Spartan methods—like sending young boys into the wilderness to survive—were extreme by today's standards, the underlying principle was to instil a sense of resilience and tenacity from a young age. Children were taught to face challenges head-on, understanding that adversity often molds the strongest characters.

We can adapt this lesson to modern parenting by encouraging our children to push their boundaries and take calculated risks. This doesn't mean putting them in dangerous situations but allowing them the freedom to fail, to learn, and to grow. Whether it's encouraging them to climb a little higher on the playground, to stand up for what they believe in, or to persist through difficulties in school, the goal is to encourage a mindset that views challenges as opportunities for growth.

By doing so, we equip our children to navigate the tumultuous seas of life, instilling in them the courage to face whatever comes their way. We teach them that they are not defined by their circumstances but by their actions and reactions. In this way, we not only prepare them for the challenges of adulthood but also contribute to the development of well-rounded, resilient individuals who can contribute positively to society.

In essence, the wisdom of ancient civilisations offers us timeless principles that can guide us in one of life's most important tasks: raising compassionate, courageous, and balanced children. While the world has changed in countless ways, the fundamental challenges and joys of parenting remain the same. By looking back, we can find enduring wisdom to guide us forward.

Ancient rituals for modern parenting

So how can we incorporate these ancient rituals into modern parenting? Here are some examples.

Storytelling Evenings
The ancient art of storytelling remains one of the most

effective ways to instil values, impart wisdom, and create a sense of community. Setting aside dedicated Storytelling Evenings can be a transformative family tradition that serves multiple purposes.

Firstly, it creates a space for quality family time, away from the distractions of screens and the outside world. Just as the Greeks gathered to hear epic tales of heroism and the Native Americans shared tribal stories around the fire, your family can come together in a dedicated space—perhaps around the dinner table or in the living room—to share stories that are meaningful to you.

Secondly, Storytelling Evenings offer an excellent platform for education and moral development. Whether you're sharing family histories that instill a sense of heritage and belonging, or folklore that teaches important life lessons, these stories serve as a unique and engaging way to encourage the values you wish to see in your children. You can even include tales from different cultures to broaden their horizons and build a sense of global citizenship.

Thirdly, it encourages active listening and imagination. In a world where information is often passively consumed, the act of listening to a story, visualising the characters, imagining the settings, can be a powerful exercise in creativity and attention for children and adults alike.

Lastly, it opens the door for meaningful conversations. After each story, encourage a discussion about its themes, the characters' choices and how they relate to your own lives. This not only enhances comprehension, but also encourages children to think critically and empathetically.

By incorporating Storytelling Evenings into your family routine, you're doing more than just entertaining your children; you're enriching their lives with the wisdom of ages past, strengthening your family bonds, and equipping them with the intellectual and emotional tools they'll need for the future.

Nature Retreats
In today's hyper-connected world, where we're often more in touch with our devices than with our inner selves, the need for genuine connection, both with nature and our own spirituality, has never been more pressing. Nature Retreats offer a modern-day solution that draws inspiration from ancient practices like the Aboriginal 'Walkabout' or the Native American 'Vision Quest.' The essence of these ancient practices was a journey into the wilderness often undertaken as a rite of passage. It was a time for deep reflection, a test of

survival skills, and a quest for visions or insights that would guide the individual through life. While we may not need to go to such extremes in our modern world the underlying principles of reflection, connection to the earth, and self-discovery remain profoundly relevant.

Nature Retreats provide a priceless chance to instill eco-conscious values in your family. With younger generations growing more concerned about the state of our planet, these retreats offer an ideal setting to incorporate lessons on sustainability and environmental stewardship. By highlighting the lasting impact of human waste and emphasizing the importance of caring for our planet, these retreats can serve as a powerful reminder of our responsibility to protect and preserve our natural world.

Nowadays people can spend a lot of time and money reconnecting with themselves and nature at organised retreats and although that is an option it doesn't have to be expensive or time-consuming. It could be as simple as a weekend camping trip or a day-long hike in the woods. The key is to make it a sacred time, free from the distractions of modern life. Leave behind your electronic devices and bring only what is necessary for survival and comfort. This is a time to connect with nature. Use this time for personal reflection and meditation. You could bring along a journal to jot down your thoughts or perhaps some spiritual or philosophical texts that inspire deep thinking.

Encourage family members to spend some time alone, contemplating their own lives, goals, and the challenges they face. This solitude, combined with the healing power of nature can offer invaluable insights. But a Nature Retreat isn't just about individual growth; it's also an opportunity for family bonding. Some of my best family holidays as a kid were camping even with the unpredictable weather. Plan activities that require teamwork, like building a fire or setting up a tent, and take board games for those wet days. Share stories and sing songs around the campfire. Teach your children basic survival skills like identifying edible plants or teaching them about the stars, imparting not just knowledge, but also a sense of responsibility and respect for nature.

By making Nature Retreats a regular family tradition, you're doing more than just taking a break from routine. You're instilling in your family a respect for the earth, a habit of self-reflection, and a deep sense of connection, both with one another and with the larger world around you. In doing so, you're not just enriching your lives, but also paying homage to the ancient wisdom that has long understood the transformative power of nature.

Rites of Passage

In many ancient civilisations, rites of passage were not just symbolic gestures, but critical tests of skill, courage, and wisdom. For example, in Maasai culture, young men were tasked with killing a lion to prove their bravery and skill as hunters. This wasn't just a test of physical prowess; it was a demonstration that the young man could protect his community from one of the most fearsome predators in their environment. The act was deeply symbolic, representing the young man's transition into a protector and provider for his community.

Similarly, in Native American cultures, young men often went on "vision quests," which were solitary journeys into the wilderness. During these quests, they would fast and seek visions to guide them in their transition to adulthood. The vision quest was not just a physical challenge, but a spiritual journey, designed to connect the individual to their inner selves and the world around them.

In ancient Sparta, young boys were sent to a rigorous military training camp known as the "agoge" at the age of seven. The training was harsh and demanding, designed to instil discipline, resilience, and martial skill. The culmination of this training was a test known as the "Krypteia," where young men were sent into the countryside armed only with a knife and were expected to survive on their own while also terrorising the local slave population. Passing this test was a rite of passage that marked the transition from boyhood to manhood.

Rites of passage were not just for the boys. In ancient Rome, girls participated in a ceremony known as the "Tusculan rite," where they would dedicate their childhood toys to the household gods as a symbolic gesture of leaving childhood behind. They would then don a "stola," the garment of Roman matrons, signifying their new status as women.

In Native American cultures, rites of passage for girls often coincided with the onset of menstruation, a natural marker of womanhood. The "Sunrise Ceremony" among the Apache, for example, is a four-day ritual that includes dancing, feasting, and various tests of physical and emotional endurance. The ceremony serves to introduce the young woman to the spiritual and social responsibilities she will take on in her community.

In some African cultures, such as the Zulu, young girls participate in "umemulo," a coming-of-age ceremony. The ritual involves a series of dances, chants, and offerings to the ancestors culminating in the slaughtering of a goat or cow to honour the young woman's transition into adulthood. The ceremony is not just a celebration, but also a public acknowledgment of the girl's readiness to take on adult responsibilities, including marriage and motherhood.

In ancient Japan young girls would go through a ceremony called "Mogi," where they would start wearing adult clothing and hairstyles, signifying their transition to womanhood. The ceremony was often accompanied by a feast and was an important social event marking the girl's eligibility for marriage.

These historical rites of passage serve as powerful examples of how societies have used rituals and tests to mark significant life transitions. While some of these practices may seem extreme or irrelevant to our modern lives, the underlying principles remain the same: rites of passage serve to instil values, skills and responsibilities that are essential for the next phase of life. By creating our own modern rites of passage we can provide our children with meaningful transformative experiences that prepare them for the challenges and responsibilities of adulthood.

In today's world, the concept of rites of passage may seem antiquated, but their essence remains relevant. These ceremonies can be adapted to fit our modern sensibilities while still serving their core purpose: to mark significant life transitions and instil a sense of responsibility and maturity. For instance, a modern adaptation could involve a wilderness retreat for both boys and girls focusing on survival skills, self-reflection and community service. Or it could be a community project that the young person plans and executes demonstrating their readiness to contribute positively to society. By incorporating these ancient rites of passage into our modern lives we offer our children meaningful markers for their journey into adulthood. We also connect them to a lineage of wisdom that has guided human development for millennia, enriching their lives with a sense of purpose and continuity.

Parenting with Purpose

In every era and across all cultures one of the most fundamental human pursuits has been the quest for purpose. This search for meaning is not just a philosophical endeavour, it has real-world implications for our happiness, well-being and sense of fulfilment. A life with purpose provides a compass that helps us navigate the complexities of existence. It's this sense of purpose that ancient civilisations so deeply understood and integrated into the very fabric of their societies especially in the realm of parenting.

In ancient societies, the task of raising children was imbued with a clarity of purpose that often seems elusive in today's complex world. From the Spartans' focus on courage and resilience to the Confucian emphasis on virtue and wisdom, each civilisation had its own set of values and virtues that were instilled in the young from an early age. Children were not just raised to survive, they were carefully groomed to uphold the values of their community, to champion virtues, and to contribute meaningfully to society.

In contrast, modern parenting often finds itself grappling with a multitude of challenges from the distractions of technology to the pressures of academic and material success. While we have made significant advancements in understanding child psychology and development there's a growing sense that something essential is missing: intentionality. This is where the wisdom of ancient civilisations can offer invaluable insights.

Mindful Rituals
One of the most potent ways to instil values in children is through the use of mindful rituals. In ancient Jewish culture, the Sabbath was not just a day of rest, but a time to reflect on the virtues of peace, gratitude and community. Similarly, Native American tribes used storytelling as a ritual to pass down the wisdom and moral lessons of their ancestors. Today modern families can create their own rituals, such as a weekly family meeting to discuss challenges and successes or a "gratitude jar" where everyone can deposit notes about what they're thankful for.

The art of discipline

What is considered acceptable in terms of discipline has changed a huge amount in my lifetime let alone across the centuries. Again the lack of physical community and therefore support makes this more difficult for parents who are navigating this on their own. In ancient societies, discipline was far from a haphazard or reactive endeavour. It was a carefully orchestrated strategy aimed at instilling the virtues and values that were the backbone of the community. Take, for example, ancient Greece where the concept of "arete" or excellence was not merely a lofty ideal, but a way of life. This was cultivated through a rigorous system of education, physical training and moral philosophy. The aim was to produce citizens who were not just knowledgeable, but also virtuous, capable of contributing to the polis (community) in meaningful ways.

In today's world discipline often gets reduced to a reactive measure, a way to correct undesirable behaviour after it has occurred. While correction is undoubtedly a part of discipline, this narrow focus misses the broader, more proactive aspect of discipline, the cultivation of virtues. After all prevention is always better than cure. Discipline should not merely be about saying "no" to bad behaviour but also about saying "yes" to the development of character. It should be a proactive approach to instilling virtues like honesty, kindness, resilience, and empathy. As a parent, I know how difficult that can be with all the other pressures we have to contend with and I am not a fan of the word should, but in this case, I am going to make an exception for what I believe we should be doing in order to do right by our own children and future civilisation.

So, how can modern parents apply this ancient wisdom? First and foremost discipline needs to be consistent. Children thrive on predictability; as it makes them feel secure. Consistency in discipline means that the rules don't change based on mood or circumstance, which helps children internalise these values more effectively.

Secondly, consider using natural consequences as a teaching tool. For instance, if a child refuses to wear a coat on a chilly day, they might get cold which will encourage them to wear the coat next time. This method teaches children to think about the consequences of their actions, a skill that will serve them well in adulthood.

Another effective technique is positive reinforcement. Celebrate and reward the behaviours that align with the virtues you're trying to instil. This could be as simple as verbal praise or as tangible as a small reward. The key is to make the child associate the virtue with positive feelings thereby encouraging its continued practice. By adopting a more proactive and intentional approach to discipline, we do more than correct immediate behaviour; we empower ourselves in disciplining our children, which removes stress from the situation. Calmer parents make for calmer children and we lay the foundation for a lifetime of virtue. We're not just raising children; we're raising future adults, who will go on to face challenges, make decisions, and contribute to their communities. And in a world that's increasingly complex and uncertain, these virtues—honesty, kindness, resilience—serve as a moral compass, guiding them toward lives of purpose and meaning.

The Conscious Cultivation of Virtues
The ancient Romans had a trio of virtues encapsulated in the phrase "Gravitas, Pietas, Dignitas," which emphasised the importance of seriousness, duty, and dignity. These virtues were not just abstract ideals they were lived experiences woven into the fabric of daily Roman life through rituals, education, and social expectations.

In our ever-changing world, the virtues we value may have evolved, but their significance remains unaltered. While the Romans prioritised duty and dignity, we now place greater emphasis on virtues such as empathy, integrity, and environmental stewardship. Yet, the fundamental principle remains unchanged: the deliberate and conscious cultivation of these virtues, seamlessly integrated into our daily lives and passed on to future generations.

The key to the successful cultivation of virtues is their integration into daily life. Virtues shouldn't be relegated to special occasions or grand gestures they should be the guiding principles that inform our actions, decisions and interactions every day. This could mean practising gratitude as a family by sharing one thing you're thankful for at dinner each night or it could mean encouraging acts of kindness, no matter how small, and recognising them when they occur will encourage more of that behaviour. As human beings, we are always motivated more by the carrot than the stick.

Raising balanced individuals
The ultimate aim of parenting, whether in the warrior society of ancient Sparta or the bustling metropolis of modern London, extends far beyond material success. It's about raising children who are rich in character and imbued with virtues like compassion, courage, and balance. These are the individuals who won't merely survive the challenges that life throws at them; they will thrive, making meaningful contributions to society in a manner that honours both their ancient heritage and their modern potential.

The foundation of this approach lies in intentionality. Intentional parenting means that every action, lesson, and moment carries a deeper purpose. It extends beyond academic achievements or athletic success; it's about instilling a moral and ethical framework that will shape their lives. This framework is built upon timeless virtues, celebrated and nurtured by civilisations throughout history. By incorporating these age-old principles into our modern parenting techniques, we offer our children something truly invaluable: a roadmap for life that is both enduring and immediately applicable. In a world of constant change, where technology and societal shifts can leave us feeling adrift, these enduring virtues act as a steadfast compass, providing a consistent guiding light in a sky that is forever shifting.

One of the most profound gifts we can give our children is a sense of purpose. Numerous studies have shown that a life lived with purpose is a life filled with happiness and fulfilment. When children understand that they're part of something bigger, that they have a role to play in the betterment of society, it instils in them a sense of worth and fulfilment that no amount of material success can provide. This is the essence of a life well-lived, a life that is rich in both meaning and joy.

Furthermore, this parenting approach places a strong emphasis on the significance of community contribution. It extends beyond personal achievements and individual growth, recognising how these virtues collectively benefit the well-being of the entire community. Whether through acts of kindness or environmental stewardship, the values we instill in our children prepare them to become engaged, accountable members of their communities.

Ultimately, our goal is to nurture well-rounded individuals. These are the kind of people who not only excel professionally, but also thrive in their personal relationships. They possess a deep understanding of emotional intelligence, gracefully navigating both triumphs and setbacks. Life's challenges are met with bravery and resilience. By instilling these virtues in our parenting approach, we go beyond preparing our children for academic trials; we prepare them for the journey of life itself. In doing so, we contribute to a legacy of compassionate courage, ethical intelligence, and a strong commitment to community well-being. These timeless values will guide our children towards lives filled with purpose, fulfillment, and meaningful contributions to society.

Chapter 10: Nurturing Masculine and Feminine Energies in Children

Today, the boundaries of gender are becoming increasingly fluid. According to recent statistics, there has been a notable rise in gender changes, signalling a societal shift towards greater acceptance of diverse identities. This new generation is embracing a more fluid understanding of gender and sexual orientation, breaking away from rigid categories that have confined us for centuries. While this progress is undoubtedly positive it also presents its own set of challenges making it crucial to raise emotionally balanced children who can navigate this complex landscape. It's essential to remember that every child—regardless of how they identify—harbours within them a unique blend of what has traditionally been categorised as 'masculine' and 'feminine' energies. These energies are not opposing forces but rather two sides of the same coin, both divine in nature. By giving our children the tools, space and understanding to balance these energies within themselves, we set the stage for them to thrive in their relationships, their families, and ultimately, in their own lives and bodies.

Ancient philosophies like Taoism and Confucianism offer us a profound framework for understanding this balance. The concept of Yin and Yang serves as a powerful metaphor for the interconnectedness and interdependence of seemingly opposite forces. In this worldview masculine and feminine energies are not in conflict, but are complementary, each one containing a seed of the other, working in harmony to create a balanced whole.

Interestingly, this wasn't a point of contention in many ancient civilisations, which often had a more nuanced understanding of gender and sexuality. The problem arose in more recent centuries when societal norms and religious doctrines began to suppress natural sexual expressions, leading to a world skewed towards masculine energies. The time has come to reclaim this lost balance and that starts with ourselves, our relationships, and how we raise our children.

So how can we, as parents, caregivers and mentors, create an environment where a child feels free to express their full range of emotions and traits? How can we ensure that our children grow up understanding that these energies are not mutually exclusive but can coexist in a balanced, harmonious way? This chapter aims to explore these questions and offer practical guidance for nurturing both masculine and feminine energies in our children irrespective of their gender.

Promote Emotional Intelligence
Emotional intelligence is a vital life skill often overlooked in traditional education. From an early age, children need to be taught not only to recognise and understand their emotions but also to effectively manage them. It's not just about navigating their internal world; it's a crucial tool for helping interpersonal relationships, achieving academic success, and ultimately thriving in their professional lives.

As a society, it is crucial to refrain from assigning gender to specific emotions and personality traits. Take empathy, for instance, often linked to feminine energy but not limited by gender. It is a universal quality that should be cultivated in all children, irrespective of their identities. Empathy empowers children to step into others' shoes, understanding their feelings and perspectives. It forms the foundation of compassion, kindness, and social harmony. We must encourage children to freely express their emotions, whether through tears when they're upset, laughter when they're happy, or articulating their feelings constructively. Only then can we address the concerning rates of suicide and violence among young men who feel unable to express themselves openly.

On the flip side, assertiveness—a trait often linked to masculine energy—is equally important. It is a critical skill that goes beyond mere self-expression; it's an anchor of emotional and psychological well-being. While society has made strides in breaking down gender norms, the importance of teaching assertiveness to all children—regardless of gender—cannot be overstated.

According to the American Psychological Association, individuals with low assertiveness levels are more likely to experience anxiety, depression, and lower life satisfaction. A study published in the Journal of Personality and Social Psychology also found that people-pleasing behaviours, often stemming from a lack of assertiveness, are linked to higher levels of stress and even long-term health
 issues.

Teaching children to stand up for themselves, voice their opinions and advocate for their needs is not about encouraging aggression; it's about instilling a sense of self-worth and the confidence to express it. This skill is invaluable in navigating life's challenges from handling peer pressure and bullying to advocating for oneself in professional settings.

Assertiveness training can start young and can be as simple as encouraging children to speak up when they disagree with something, ask for what they need, or say no when something makes them uncomfortable. These exercises lay the groundwork for more complex life scenarios, such as negotiating, setting boundaries, and standing up against injustice.

By teaching assertiveness, we're not just preparing children for the confrontations they'll inevitably face; we're also protecting them from the long-term emotional and psychological repercussions of passivity. We're empowering them to take control of their lives, to set and maintain boundaries, and to engage with the world in a way that respects both themselves and others.

By instilling both empathy and assertiveness in our children, we're not just preparing them for the tests of school, but for the tests of life. We're raising individuals who are emotionally intelligent, balanced in their masculine and feminine energies and equipped to thrive in an increasingly complex world.

Diversify Play
Toys and games serve as more than mere distractions or entertainment for children. They are foundational tools that help shape a child's worldview, skills and emotional intelligence. From the moment they grasp their first toy children begin to explore the boundaries of their imagination, the limits of physics, and the basics of human interaction. In this context, the importance of diversifying the types of toys and games available to children cannot be overstated.

By offering a well-rounded toy chest that includes everything from dolls and kitchen sets to trucks and building blocks we give children the opportunity to explore a broad spectrum of activities. This variety promotes diverse skills, from empathy and caregiving (often associated with dolls) to spatial awareness and problem-solving (commonly linked to building blocks and puzzles). It's not just about breaking down gender stereotypes, although that's a significant benefit, it's about equipping children with a more comprehensive set of life skills.

Letting children lead the way in their play preferences is crucial. When we allow them to choose freely we send a powerful message, their interests are valid, irrespective of societal norms. This freedom of choice encourages self-expression and can be incredibly liberating for a child who may already feel the societal pressures of conforming to gender roles. Avoiding the categorisation of toys and games into 'for boys' or 'for girls', is not just a politically correct move, it's a conscious effort to broaden our children's horizons and skill sets. By doing so, we're not just raising boys who can cook or girls who can build,
we're raising a generation of well-rounded, emotionally intelligent individuals who understand that their abilities are not confined by their gender.

In a world where we are becoming more reliant on emotional intelligence, creativity, and problem-solving, diversifying play is not just a nice idea—it's a necessity to thrive. It's about preparing our children for a future where the balance of 'masculine' and 'feminine' skills will be even more intertwined, both in the workplace and in interpersonal relationships. So the next time you find yourself in the toy aisle, remember: you're not just buying a toy; you're investing in your child's future.

Encourage a Variety of Friendships
Friendships are a foundation of emotional well-being and personal development. While family lays the emotional foundation, friendships offer a dynamic arena for children to explore their identities, test interpersonal skills, and mature emotionally. In this context, the traditional notion of steering children towards friendships within their own gender group is increasingly outdated. Such an approach perpetuates gender stereotypes and limits the emotional and social range that children can experience.

Today's society is rapidly evolving, with a more liberal understanding of gender roles and identity. The next generation is notably more fluid in their approach to sexuality and relationships, challenging the traditional norms that many of us were raised with. In this changing landscape, encouraging diverse friendships—across genders, cultures, and even age groups—is not just progressive, but essential. It equips children with the emotional and social dexterity they'll need in a world that values both individuality and collaboration. For example, a boy with close friendships with girls may find it easier to express emotions and practice empathy, traits often unfairly labelled as feminine. Conversely, a girl with friendships among boys may be encouraged to be more assertive and take risks, traits traditionally considered masculine. These friendships also offer children different perspectives on problem-solving, conflict resolution, and emotional support, enriching their own approaches to life's challenges.

Beyond gender, friendships should also span various cultural backgrounds, interests, and abilities. This not only broadens a child's worldview but also instils values of inclusivity and respect for differences, virtues increasingly important in our globalised society.

Let's explore the innate human longing for connection on a profound level. Beyond our diverse friendships, there exists the concept of discovering our "tribe" - a tightly-knit community that nourishes us emotionally and provides a sense of belonging. This inherent need to belong is deeply ingrained in our psychology and plays a vital role in our emotional well-being. Within a tribe, children learn the value of loyalty, shared experiences, and the emotional depth that blossoms from genuine, meaningful connections.
In a world where issues like loneliness and social isolation are increasingly prevalent, and further fueled by gender stereotypes and societal norms, the quest to find our tribe has never been more crucial. It serves

as a sanctuary where children can freely express their authentic selves, absorbing a myriad of qualities and skills from individuals who truly comprehend and celebrate them.

Exemplify Balanced Energies
Being a parent is wonderful, hard work and at times terrifying especially when you realise the immense influence you have as role models to your children. It terrifies me and I coach parents for a living. All children are a product of their environment. It is nature v nurture which, as parents, we have all experienced the fact that Children do as they see, not as they're told. When it comes to nurturing balanced masculine and feminine energies in our children, our own behaviour serves as the most potent lesson.

In a previous chapter, we delved into the importance of balancing your own energies, both within yourself and in your relationship with your partner. This balance is not just for the health of your relationship or personal well-being; it's also a living, breathing lesson for your children. When they see their fathers openly express vulnerability or their mothers make assertive, confident decisions, they internalise these behaviours as normal and acceptable, irrespective of gender.

Based on my personal experiences as a child of divorce and later as a divorcee myself, I can firmly affirm the profound impact that our parents' relationship dynamics have on us. This influence extends to my siblings as well, as four out of my five brothers and sisters have also experienced divorce. The environment in which we are raised plays a pivotal role in shaping our attitudes towards relationships, conflict, and even our own self-worth. Numerous studies have consistently highlighted that children of divorced parents are more likely to go through divorce themselves. For instance, Nicholas Wolfinger's study revealed that children of divorced parents face a 40% higher likelihood of getting divorced compared to those with married parents. This recurring cycle emphasises the critical importance of setting a balanced and harmonious example for our children to follow.

So, how can you consciously exemplify this balance? It starts with self-awareness and a commitment to personal growth. Take for example Sarah and Will, parents to Emma, 8 and Joshua, 14. They initially sought coaching due to concerns about Joshua's emotional well-being. Joshua had been experiencing frequent emotional outbursts at school, leading to disciplinary actions and strained relationships with his peers. His teachers and school counsellors were concerned, and the Thompsons knew they needed professional guidance. However, through our coaching sessions, it became apparent that Emma was also struggling, albeit in a less overt way. She had been withdrawing from social activities and was reluctant to voice her opinions in class, showing signs of low self-esteem. While Joshua's issues were the immediate trigger for seeking help, it was clear that the entire family dynamic needed to be addressed.

Sarah and Will engaged in individual and couples coaching sessions to explore their own masculine and feminine energies. They also participated in mindfulness practices and open communication exercises to better understand each other's needs and feelings.

Sarah and Will focused on balancing the masculine and feminine energies within their relationship. They began communicating more openly with each other and as a family, sharing responsibilities and activities within the home. They also engaged in mindfulness practices and redefined boundaries to model a balanced relationship for their children. They also diversified the children's play and activities, encouraging both Emma and Joshua to explore different facets of their personalities.

As a result of these small changes, Joshua's emotional outbursts significantly decreased, and he became more open about discussing his feelings, leading to a more stable emotional state and improved relationships at school. Emma, who had been quietly struggling, began to come out of her shell. She became more confident, willing to take risks, and started voicing her opinions more freely, both at home and in school. Her self-esteem improved dramatically.

As for Sarah and Will, they found a newfound balance in their relationship, breaking free from the limiting gender roles that had confined them. By consciously choosing to embody a balanced blend of masculine and feminine energies, Sarah and Will not only improved their own relationship but also set a powerful example for their children. They showed Emma and Joshua that they could be multi-dimensional individuals unconfined by societal norms about gender and behaviour. In doing so, they laid the foundation for their children's emotional and relational well-being, setting them up for healthier, more balanced relationships in their adult lives.

Whether it's through mindfulness practices, relationship coaching, or simply open and honest communication with your partner, the goal is to cultivate a relationship and personal demeanour that embodies these diverse energies. Show your children that it's okay for anyone to cry and express emotions, just as it's okay to stand up for what you believe in. In doing so, you're not just improving your own quality of life, you're laying the foundation for your children's emotional and relational well-being. You're teaching them that they don't have to be confined by societal norms and expectations regarding gender and behaviour. Instead, they can embrace a fuller, more balanced range of human experience, setting them up for healthier, more harmonious relationships in their own adult lives.

Open Dialogues
Engaging in candid conversations about feelings, ambitions, fears, and dreams creates a safe space where children can explore the full spectrum of human emotion and aspiration. When children understand that it's okay to be both nurturing and strong, intuitive and logical, they become more well-rounded individuals, better equipped to navigate the complexities of modern life.
In today's digital age, where so much communication happens online, often with people we've never met, teaching our children effective communication skills is more critical than ever. They need to know how to articulate their thoughts and feelings clearly, how to listen and ask questions, and perhaps most importantly, how to ask for help when they need it. These skills are not just essential for their immediate well-being but are foundational for their future happiness and fulfilment.

Alongside open dialogue the stories we expose our children to play a significant role in shaping their perceptions. Whether it's through books, movies, or oral narratives, featuring characters that embrace both masculine and feminine energies can have a lasting impact. For example, a story about a female scientist who solves problems through both logical reasoning and empathetic understanding can send a powerful message. Similarly, a tale of a male caregiver who uses both strength and sensitivity to navigate challenges can be equally impactful.

By combining open conversations with balanced narratives, we're doing more than just breaking down gender stereotypes; we're equipping our children with the emotional and intellectual tools they need to lead balanced, fulfilling lives. We're teaching them that communication is not just a skill, but a lifeline, a means through which they can connect, understand, and be understood, in a world that desperately needs more of that.

Teach Resilience and Compassion
Resilience and compassion are often viewed as separate qualities, each belonging to a different end of the masculine-feminine energy spectrum. However the true beauty lies in their harmonious coexistence within an individual. Teaching our children to embody both resilience and compassion is not just about preparing them for the challenges and joys of life; it's about setting the stage for a more balanced, empathetic, and effective future generation.
Take, for example, a situation where a child witnesses bullying. Teaching them to stand up for the bullied

friend instils resilience, a quality often associated with masculine energy. This act requires courage, assertiveness, and a sense of justice. On the other hand, encouraging the same child to understand and feel for the bully cultivates compassion, a trait commonly linked to feminine energy. This requires empathy, emotional intelligence, and a nuanced understanding that negative behaviour often arises from personal struggles.

By nurturing both these energies in our children, we're equipping them with a holistic set of skills and values that will serve them well in all areas of life—from personal relationships to professional endeavours. More importantly, we're contributing to the collective effort to bring about a "Golden Age," a future where individuals are not just successful in a material sense, but are also emotionally intelligent, socially responsible, and spiritually aware.
In a world that is increasingly polarised, the ability to be both strong and kind, to stand up for what's right while also seeking to understand, will be the pillar of a more harmonious society. These are the individuals who will lead with both head and heart, who will build bridges where there are divides and who will embody the balanced, integrated energies that promise a brighter, more enlightened future.

Celebrate Individuality

In a world that frequently seeks to categorise and assign labels, it is imperative to remember that every child is a distinctive amalgamation of qualities, passions, and energies. While societal expectations have traditionally dictated that boys should embody toughness and girls should embrace nurturing qualities, these outdated constraints fail to acknowledge the intricacies of the human experience.

Some boys may naturally gravitate towards activities or traits traditionally considered "feminine," such as nurturing, caregiving, or artistic expression. Similarly, some girls may show a strong inclination for what are often considered "masculine" traits, like assertiveness, problem-solving, or physical strength. This individuality should not only be accepted but celebrated.

By allowing children the freedom to explore their interests and express their personalities without the burden of societal expectations we empower them to become more well-rounded individuals. This is not just about breaking gender stereotypes; it's about acknowledging and honouring the full range of human capabilities and emotions.

When we celebrate this individuality we send a powerful message to our children that they are valued for who they are, not for how well they fit into preconceived roles. This creates a sense of self-worth and confidence that will serve them well throughout their lives, enabling them to engage more authentically with the world around them.

By encouraging this kind of individual expression, we're also laying the groundwork for a more inclusive, equitable society, one where people are recognised and valued for their unique contributions, rather than being confined by limiting stereotypes. In the long run, this not only benefits our children, but enriches our communities and society as a whole.

In conclusion, the formative years of a child's life present a golden opportunity to instil a balanced understanding of masculine and feminine energies. Far from being opposing forces, these energies are complementary facets of the human experience. By consciously creating an environment that encourages emotional fluidity and breaks free from the constraints of traditional gender roles we are laying a robust foundation for the next generation.

In a world grappling with inequality, division, and a lack of emotional intelligence, raising children who embody both masculine and feminine energies is not only a parenting strategy but a societal imperative. It becomes our social responsibility to nurture balanced individuals who appreciate the inherent strengths of both energies and harmoniously integrate them. This balanced perspective has profound implications. It equips our children to navigate the complexities of modern relationships, workplace dynamics, and global challenges with a nuanced, empathetic approach. It prepares them for a future that is not just technologically advanced, but emotionally intelligent, not just globally connected, but deeply compassionate.

Furthermore, creating a well-rounded upbringing will contribute to a societal transformation, marked by increased inclusivity, understanding, and holistic well-being. As these children grow to become the leaders, policymakers, and parents of tomorrow, their comprehensive approach to life and human interaction will lay the foundation for a more harmonious and equitable world. In essence, by nurturing both masculine and feminine energies in our children today, we are investing in a future that holds the promise of balance, inclusivity, and harmony. A future that embraces and celebrates the full spectrum of human potential.

Chapter 11: Rituals and Practices for Modern Couples

Throughout history, the need for love and connection between couples has been nurtured through rituals and practices. From the sacred rites of ancient Egypt to the spiritual ceremonies of Native American tribes. These rituals have served as both anchors and compasses. They have provided couples with a framework to navigate the unpredictable seas of life, fortifying their bonds against the storms of time, circumstance, and change.

Today relationships are increasingly complex and often fraught with challenges—from the erosion of intimacy due to digital distractions to the dissolution of traditional roles and expectations—these ancient rituals take on renewed significance. They offer us a roadmap, a set of time-tested coordinates that can guide modern couples towards deeper intimacy, mutual understanding, and enduring love.

But the question arises: How can we adapt these ancient practices to fit the unique contours of contemporary relationships? How can we take the essence of these rituals, steeped in cultural and spiritual wisdom, and apply them in a way that resonates with our modern sensibilities?

This chapter aims to bridge that gap, offering a curated selection of rituals and practices that are rooted in ancient wisdom yet tailored to the needs and realities of today's couples. Whether you're seeking to reignite the spark in a long-term relationship, deepen the emotional connection in a new romance, or simply maintain the vibrant energy of an already fulfilling partnership, these rituals offer practical, meaningful ways to enrich your love life.
So, let's embark on this journey together, exploring how the wisdom of the past can illuminate the path to love and connection in the present and future.

Rekindling the Sacred Fire: Ancient Rituals
In many ancient cultures fire was more than just a source of warmth and light; it was a potent symbol of passion, transformation, and divine energy. From the Vedic Yajna ceremonies in ancient India to the Celtic Beltane fires rituals involving the lighting and tending of a sacred flame were not just communal events but intimate ceremonies that honoured the divine union between couples. These fires served as a physical manifestation of the spiritual and emotional bonds that connected them, a glowing testament to the enduring nature of their love.

In our fast-paced, digitally-driven world, the need for such grounding rituals has never been greater. So, how can we adapt this ancient practice to our modern lives? The answer is surprisingly simple and yet profoundly impactful. Set aside a regular evening, perhaps once a week or even once a month, specifically dedicated to you and your partner. During this time light a candle together allowing it to symbolise the eternal flame of your love and commitment. As you both sit in the soft glow of its flickering light take a moment to disconnect from the distractions of the outside world. Turn off your phones, shut down your computers, and give each other the gift of undivided attention.

Use this sacred time to discuss your hopes, dreams, and challenges. Share your fears and your triumphs, your uncertainties and your aspirations. This isn't just idle chatter; it's a deliberate act of emotional and spiritual communion. As you speak and listen let the candle's flame serve as a visual reminder of the warmth and light you bring to each other's lives.

This modern adaptation of an ancient ritual serves multiple purposes. It not only enables open communication but also creates a space for emotional intimacy. It allows you both to pause and reflect on your relationship, to honour its strengths and acknowledge its challenges. Most importantly, it serves as a regular reaffirmation of your love and

commitment, a tangible ritual that feeds the sacred fire of your union.
So, light that candle and in doing so rekindle the sacred fire that burns at the heart of your love. Let it illuminate your path as a couple, guiding you through the complexities of modern life with the wisdom of ancient rituals.

The Dance of Yin and Yang: Balance & Harmony
In ancient Chinese philosophy, the concept of Yin and Yang represents the dual nature of existence. Yin is often associated with qualities like receptivity, nurturing, and introspection, while Yang is linked to action, assertiveness, and outward focus. For couples in ancient China understanding the interplay of these energies within their relationship was not just philosophical musings, but practical wisdom. It was a way to ensure fluidity, mutual respect, and a deep understanding between partners. The dance of Yin and Yang was, and still is, a dance of balance and harmony.

In today's world, where the hustle and bustle often drown out moments of quiet introspection, the need for balance in our relationships is more crucial than ever. One way to integrate this ancient wisdom into modern relationships is through the practice of 'Yin and Yang' days.

Allocate time each month, perhaps one weekend or even just a day, for what you'll call a 'Yin Day.' On this day, the focus is on activities that nourish both the body and the soul. Think of activities that are nurturing, introspective, and calming. This could mean meditating together in the morning, taking a nature walk in the afternoon and perhaps ending the day with a joint journaling session where you both write down what you're grateful for or what you've learned about each other and yourselves.

On the flip side, designate another day as a 'Yang Day.' These days are about action, about harnessing that outward-focused, assertive energy. Engage in activities that get your blood pumping and your mind working. This could mean participating in a competitive sport, going on an adventurous hike, brainstorming future plans, or diving into a challenging hobby that you can learn and enjoy together.

The beauty of these Yin and Yang days is that they offer a structured yet flexible way to ensure that both energies are honoured and cultivated in your relationship. It's a proactive approach to maintaining balance, inviting both introspection and action into your lives.

By consciously dedicating time to nurture these different aspects, you're not just doing activities together; you're also deepening your understanding of each other and of the energies that make you both unique and complementary. You're learning to dance the ancient dance of Yin and Yang, and in doing so, you're creating a relationship that is both balanced and harmonious, deeply rooted in ancient wisdom yet perfectly tailored for the complexities of modern life.

Ceremonies of Renewal
In ancient civilisations like those of the Egyptians and Mayans, ceremonies of renewal were deeply ingrained in the fabric of marital life. These weren't just one-off events. but recurring rituals that allowed couples to pause, reflect, and reaffirm their commitment to each other. They served as vital touchpoints in the relationship, opportunities to celebrate milestones, honour mutual growth and rekindle the vision for the future.

While renewing marriage vows is becoming increasingly popular in contemporary society, the concept of renewal doesn't have to be limited to grand ceremonies or significant anniversaries. It can be a more regular and intimate affair, tailored to the unique dynamics of your relationship. Consider establishing your own 'Day of Renewal,' which could be your wedding anniversary, the day you first met, or any other date that holds special meaning for you both. On this day, take time to express gratitude for each other and the journey you've shared so far. Reflect on the highs and lows, the challenges overcome, and the joys experienced. Renew your commitments or even introduce new vows that resonate with your evolving relationship and individual growth. You could make this as elaborate or as simple as you like. It could involve a weekend getaway, a special dinner, or even just a quiet evening at home with a bottle of wine. The key is to make it a sacred time, free from the distractions of daily life, where you can focus solely on each other.

By incorporating this modern take on an ancient practice, you're not just keeping the spark alive, you're fanning the flames of a love that grows stronger, deeper, and more resilient with each passing year.

Moonlit Conversations
In ancient cultures, the moon was more than just a celestial body; it was a sacred symbol imbued with divine energy. Among the Maoris of New Zealand, for instance, the moon was believed to be a facilitator of deep meaningful communication. Couples would sit under its luminous glow to share their deepest fears, joys and aspirations, trusting that the moon's energy would bless their union with clarity and understanding.

Drawing inspiration from this ancient wisdom, consider making moonlit conversations a regular practice in your relationship. Every full moon, or even once during each supermoon, take a stroll with your partner under the night sky. Let the moon's serene glow serve as a backdrop for heart-to-heart conversations that go beyond the surface level.

As I shared in Chapter 3, understanding the lunar cycles can help you tap into the divine feminine energy that the moon represents. Use this time to dive deep into each other's souls, leaving behind the hustle and distractions of daily life. Discuss your dreams, fears and aspirations and allow the moon's energy to infuse your relationship with a sense of peace and clarity.
By incorporating this ritual into your relationship, you're not just enjoying a romantic evening, you're also creating a sacred space for emotional and spiritual connection. It's an opportunity to pause, reflect, and truly see each other, fortified by the same celestial energy that has guided lovers for millennia.

The Hourglass Ritual
Time is one of the most precious commodities we have and ancient civilisations were acutely aware of its fleeting nature. Hourglasses or sand clocks were more than just timekeeping devices; they were profound symbols that reminded people of the transient nature of life. In relationships, they served as a poignant reminder to cherish each moment and make the most of the time spent together.
Modern Take: The Unplugged Hourglass Evening

In today's fast-paced, digitally saturated world, the need to disconnect and focus on the present moment is more crucial than ever. To bring the wisdom of the hourglass into your modern relationship, consider dedicating an "Hourglass Evening" every so often.

Here's how it works: Flip an hourglass and spend that hour completely unplugged from all digital distractions. No phones, no tablets, no TV—just you and your partner, fully present in the moment. You could use this time to engage in meaningful conversation, dance to your favourite songs, cook a meal together, or simply sit in each other's company, absorbing the silence or the sounds of nature.
The aim is to make that hour a sacred space, a testament to the gift of time you give each other. It's an opportunity to slow down, to appreciate the simple yet profound joy of being together, and to consciously invest in your relationship. As the sands in the hourglass run out, you'll find that the quality of time spent far outweighs the quantity, leaving you both enriched and more deeply connected.

Reconnecting with nature
In our modern, hyper-connected world, it's easy to lose touch with the natural rhythms that once guided our lives and relationships. To reconnect, consider embarking on periodic 'nature retreats' with your partner. These retreats serve as a contemporary

solution, drawing inspiration from ancient practices like the Aboriginal 'Walkabout' or the Native American 'Vision Quest' – journeys into the wilderness for profound reflection and connection with the Earth. Whether it's a weekend camping trip in the mountains, a day spent by the ocean, or even a simple picnic in a local park, the goal is to immerse yourselves in the natural world. Leave behind your electronic devices and allow nature's captivating beauty to envelop you. Feel the soil beneath your feet, listen to the rustling leaves, observe the wildlife, and gaze at the stars. Utilise this time for personal reflection, journaling, or even meditative practices that you can do as a couple.

However, nature retreats offer more than just individual growth; they provide an opportunity for relationship growth as well. Plan activities that require teamwork, such as building a fire or setting up a tent. Share stories and perhaps even renew your vows in a natural setting, with the Earth as your witness.
By making these nature retreats a regular part of your relationship, you're doing more than simply taking a break from routine. You're reconnecting with the Earth and with each other, instilling in your relationship a profound respect for the natural world and creating a deep sense of shared purpose and connection. In doing so, you're not only enriching your lives but also paying homage to the ancient wisdom that has long understood the transformative power of nature.

Prioritising Your Relationship

Life can get overwhelmingly busy, with all the noise and chaos making it easy to lose sight of the core relationship that serves as the foundation for everything else: your partnership. Amidst work commitments, raising children, and managing the household, the intimate connection between you and your partner sometimes takes a back seat. However, as we've discussed before, nurturing your relationship can be the Keystone of a balanced and harmonious life for both you and your family.

Carving out sacred space in your week dedicated solely to your relationship is not a luxury—it's a necessity. This is a precious time to check in with each other, cultivate intimacy, share vulnerabilities, and connect on a deep emotional level. This sacred space acts as a sanctuary, shielding you from the distractions and demands of the outside world. Choose a specific day and time that works for both of you, marking it on your calendars as an unbreakable appointment.

Create an environment that encourages intimacy—light a candle, play soft music, or simply sit in a quiet room. The key is to eliminate distractions: turn off your phones, ensure the kids are taken care of, and focus solely on each other.

Set some ground rules for example:
- Focused Conversation: This time is only about your relationship, your emotional needs, and your connection. No talk about kids, work, or life admin is allowed unless it's about seeking emotional support for an issue that's affecting your well-being.
- Be Open and Vulnerable: This is a safe space. Share your fears, your dreams, your insecurities, and your triumphs. The more open you are the deeper the connection you'll forge.
- No life admin: Schedule a separate time in the week to discuss life admin, finances, and other practical matters. Keep the sacred space exclusively for nurturing your emotional and intimate connection.

Here are some practical steps to include in this ritual:

- Begin by asking each other simple questions like, "How are you feeling?" or "What's been on your mind this week?" Listen attentively and respond thoughtfully.
- Share something that you haven't shared before. It could be a fear you're grappling with or a dream you're hesitant to vocalise. The idea is to peel back the layers and reveal your true self.

- Engage in a short, guided meditation or simply hold hands and take deep breaths together. Visualise your energies intertwining, creating a harmonious union.
- End the ritual by affirming your love for each other and discussing one thing you're looking forward to doing together in the coming week.

Like any ritual, the power lies in consistency. The more regularly you engage in this practice, the more natural it will become, and the deeper your connection will grow. When you are constantly being pulled in different directions, this sacred space can serve as your anchor, keeping your relationship strong, fulfilling and resilient.

By prioritising your relationship in this intentional way, you're not just enriching your own life. but also setting a powerful example for your children and those around you. You're showing them that love, like any other precious thing in life, requires care, attention, and above all time.

Rituals are not mere symbolic acts, but powerful tools for transformation. They serve as bridges between our past and present, between our spiritual selves and our daily lives, and most importantly, between our hearts and the hearts of those we love.

Incorporating rituals into your relationship doesn't just add a layer of depth and meaning, it creates a framework for intentional living and loving. It's a way to say, "This relationship matters to me, and I'm willing to invest in it." Whether it's lighting a candle to honour your eternal flame, engaging in 'Yin and Yang' days to balance energies, or setting aside sacred time each week to connect deeply, each ritual serves as a touchstone for your relationship—a constant reminder of its significance and beauty.

These rituals aren't static; they evolve as you do, reflecting the growth and changes in your relationship. They can be adapted, modified, and even replaced as you navigate different phases of your life together. The key is to keep the essence intact: a dedicated effort to honour, celebrate, and nurture the love you share.
In a world that often feels chaotic and unpredictable, rituals offer a sense of stability and continuity. They are both an anchor and a sail, grounding us and propelling us forward. As you integrate these age-old practices into your relationship, you'll find that they not only enrich your relationship, but also deepen your understanding of each other and yourselves.

Chapter 12: Enduring Love

The intricacies of human relationships is created through our emotions, experiences, and memories.

Every relationship is unique.. Yet, there is a universal truth that resonates through time and culture, love requires nurturing. The ancient civilisations might not have had the distractions of modern technology or the pressures of contemporary life, but they had their own challenges. Still, they managed to etch stories of love so profound that they echo down through the ages, reaching us today. They understood something essential— that love is an ever-evolving dance. A dance that needs space, understanding, and above all, intention.

Your relationship, with all its modern complexities, is no different from those ancient tales at its core. It yearns for understanding, craves deep connection, and thrives on mutual respect. The lessons from the ancients are not mere stories, but tools. Tools that you can use to carve out your own everlasting tale.

So, where do you go from here? Here are some practical takeaways you can use to elevate your relationship to new and exciting heights and make your life and love truly extraordinary.

Reflection and Intention

Reflection and intention serve as the compass points that guide your relationship through its journey, helping you navigate both calm seas and stormy waters. The act of reflection is not merely a nostalgic glance back at your shared history; it's an essential practice that allows you to understand the dynamics that have shaped your relationship. By examining the highs and lows, the triumphs and challenges, you gain invaluable insights into the patterns that have emerged over time. This retrospective view can reveal the strengths that have kept you together during tough times and the vulnerabilities that may require attention and care.

But reflection alone is not enough. It must be paired with the intention to give your relationship direction and purpose. Setting intentions is like plotting a course on a map. These intentions aren't just goals or milestones you want to reach; they are the values and principles that you both agree will guide your relationship into the future. Whether it's a commitment to better communication, a promise to prioritise quality time, or a mutual desire to contribute positively to each other's lives, these intentions set the tone for the next phase of your relationship journey.

The beauty of combining reflection with intention is that it creates a dynamic, living framework for your relationship. It's not a one-time exercise but a continual process that evolves with you. And the guiding force behind this practice should always be mutual respect, understanding, and love. These core values ensure that your intentions are aligned with the highest good for both partners, setting the stage for a relationship that is not just enduring but also enriching.

So, as you navigate the complexities and joys of your relationship, make time for this practice of reflection and intention. It's a gift you give not just to each other, but also to the relationship itself. A gift that keeps on giving, fortifying your bond and deepening your connection with each passing year.

Adopt Rituals
The rituals and practices outlined in previous chapters are far more than mere historical recounts or theoretical concepts; they are actionable tasks designed to enrich your relationship in tangible ways. They offer a structured way to infuse your relationship with meaning, intention, and connection, turning ordinary moments into sacred experiences.

For example, setting aside time for deep, meaningful conversations isn't just about improving communication; it's about creating a ritual of emotional intimacy. This dedicated time becomes a sanctuary where both partners can be heard, understood, and valued. Similarly, the practice of expressing gratitude toward each other isn't merely a nice gesture; it's a ritual that create a culture of appreciation and respect within the relationship. It serves as a constant reminder of the qualities and actions that make your partner special, reinforcing the positive dynamics that contribute to a healthy, loving relationship.

Celebrating milestones, whether it's anniversaries, achievements, or even overcoming challenges, is another ritual that adds depth and richness to your partnership. These celebrations serve as markers on your relationship journey, moments where you can pause, reflect, and honour the path you've walked together. They offer an opportunity to acknowledge growth, resilience and the shared experiences that have shaped your relationship.

Incorporating rituals into your relationship doesn't have to be complicated or time-consuming. It's about making a conscious choice to elevate certain actions or practices into meaningful rituals. The key is consistency and mutual engagement. When both partners actively participate, these rituals become a keystone of your relationship, a set of shared experiences that you return to time and again to nourish your emotional and spiritual connection.

So, as you continue to explore the practices discussed in this book, consider how you can adopt them as rituals in your own relationship. Make them an integral part of your life together and watch how they transform not just individual moments, but the very essence of your partnership.

Commit to Growth

In the same way that ancient civilisations meticulously constructed monumental structures, brick by brick, consider your relationship as a monument you're building together—a living testament to your love, commitment, and shared experiences. The key to this monumental endeavour is a mutual commitment to growth. Just as a monument requires regular maintenance and sometimes even renovations to stand the test of time, your relationship too needs continual nurturing and intentional development.

Committing to growth can take various forms each adding a unique layer of strength and resilience to your relationship. For instance, seeking knowledge through books, articles, or even relationship coaching can provide you with the tools and insights needed to navigate the complexities of love and partnership. As a relationship coach, I offer a range of services designed to facilitate this kind of growth, from digital products that you can engage with at your own pace, to more intensive couples' workshops that provide hands-on strategies for improving your relationship.

Being open to change and evolution is another crucial aspect of growth. Relationships are dynamic; they're not meant to be static entities, but evolving partnerships that adapt to each phase of life. This could mean being open to new experiences, whether it's travelling to new places, trying out new hobbies, or even exploring spiritual practices that bring you closer as a couple. My kin app, for example, serves as a hub for couples looking to grow together, offering a variety of resources that cater to different aspects of relationship development.

Another avenue for growth is attending couples' workshops or retreats. These experiences offer a concentrated period where you can focus solely on each other, often providing breakthrough moments that can take your relationship to the next level. I offer retreats that not only focus on the relationship between you and your partner but also delve into the relationship you have with yourself, which is the foundation for any healthy partnership. The commitment to growth is an ongoing process, one that requires both partners to be actively engaged. It's not a one-off event, but a continuous journey. By regularly checking in with each other, perhaps through a monthly review, you assess how well each of your needs are being met, you can identify areas that require attention and strategize on how to support each other in those aspects.

So, as you continue to lay each brick of your relationship monument, remember that each layer represents a chapter of growth, a story of overcoming, and a testament to your enduring love. Commit to growing together, and your monument will not only stand the test of time but will also serve as an inspiring beacon for others navigating the intricate landscapes of love and commitment.

Become a Conscious Lover

The term "conscious uncoupling" which gained widespread attention when Gwyneth Paltrow and Chris Martin used it to describe their amicable divorce. Their approach advocated for a respectful and mindful separation, particularly for the sake of their children. As a relationship coach who has guided many couples, especially parents, through the process of conscious uncoupling, I can attest to the value of bringing awareness and intentionality to the end of a relationship. However, what I advocate for is taking that same level of consciousness and applying it at the beginning and throughout the course of a relationship. I call this "conscious coupling." Don't get me wrong we are living longer and until death do us part carries far more weight than it once did, we change over time and sometimes drifting apart is inevitable. Or sometimes we were never really compatible in the first place, and were just swept up in the emotions. I have been there myself in my first marriage. I know now we were never really compatible, I just didn't want to disappoint everyone by calling off the wedding. It was a very expensive mistake to make. However I have also worked with couples who are divorcing, but with some conscious effort earlier on could have saved their marriages and thrived together as a couple.

In a world that has become more interconnected yet paradoxically more transactional, the stakes for meaningful relationships are higher than ever. We live in an era where our expectations and opportunities have outpaced those of previous generations. We're told that marriage takes work, but how many of us are genuinely prepared to put in the effort, especially when the world offers us an array of options and distractions?

To be an extraordinary partner in this complex landscape you must bring a heightened level of consciousness to your relationship. This means showing up every day as the best lover you can be, the kind of partner you would want to be with. My best advice is to write a list of all the attributes and qualities you want from a partner and then strive to be that person. It's about being intentional in your actions, thoughtful in your conversations, and committed to mutual growth and understanding. That does not mean you have to be perfect, we are human after all, we all have off days, but you do have to take responsibility for your side of the street and work at being the best you can be and taking necessary action.

Conscious coupling goes beyond the honeymoon phase; it's a continual practice of checking in with each other, setting mutual goals, and being transparent about your needs and desires. It's about creating a life that both of you love, not just coexisting.

This practice is not just for the benefit of your relationship but also serves as a model for the next generation. Children learn about relationships by observing their parents. By practising conscious coupling, you're not just enhancing your own relationship; you're contributing to a legacy of healthier, more fulfilling relationships for future generations.

So, as you navigate the intricacies of love and commitment, remember that becoming a conscious lover isn't a destination but a journey—one that requires ongoing effort, mutual respect, and a shared vision for the future. In doing so, you're not just working on your relationship; you're elevating it to an extraordinary level, setting the stage for a fulfilling union that stands the test of time.

Learn the Language of Love

In an age where we have unprecedented access to information and insights into human behaviour, it's crucial to use this knowledge to empower our relationships. One of the most transformative ways to do this is by understanding the concept of love languages. Developed by Dr Gary Chapman, the Five Love Languages theory posits that each of us has a primary way we express and interpret love: Words of

Affirmation, Acts of Service, Receiving Gifts, Quality Time, and Physical Touch.

Understanding your love language, as well as that of your partner and children if you have them, can be a game-changer for your relationship. It's like being handed a manual to your partner's emotional needs and desires, and vice versa. For instance, if your partner's primary love language is 'Words of Affirmation,' a simple compliment or word of encouragement can make their day. On the other hand, if 'Acts of Service' speak to them, helping with chores or cooking a meal can be incredibly meaningful.

But it's not just about knowing these languages; it's about consciously applying them in your daily life. This means taking deliberate actions to show love in the way your partner best understands it. If your love language is 'Quality Time,' carve out moments in your busy schedule to spend uninterrupted time together. If it's 'Physical Touch,' a hug or a simple touch on the arm can convey volumes.

And this doesn't just apply to romantic relationships. If you have children, understanding their love languages can help you connect with them on a deeper level, setting the foundation for a lifetime of healthy emotional interactions. It can also be a valuable tool for resolving conflicts and misunderstandings, as you'll have a better grasp of what each person in the relationship truly needs to feel loved and valued.

In this age of technological advancement, despite being more interconnected than ever, we find ourselves grappling with increased feelings of loneliness, depression, and anxiety. However, there is a simple solution – learning and applying the language of love. By harnessing the vast wealth of knowledge available at our fingertips, we can enrich our most intimate relationships, forging bonds that are not only robust but also profoundly fulfilling.

Show Compassion

Compassion goes beyond being an emotional response; it is a fundamental principle that should guide how you approach life and relationships. When you commit to practicing compassion, it's not just about being kinder; it lays the foundation for more fulfilling and harmonious relationships with your partner and everyone else in your life, including your children.

Compassion is an active choice, a commitment to seeing the good intentions in your partner even when their actions may suggest otherwise. It provides a lens through which you can view disagreements as opportunities for deeper understanding and connection, rather than as threats. When you embrace compassion as a way of being, you're essentially saying, "I choose to see you for your intentions, not just your actions. I choose understanding over judgment." The beauty of compassion is that it works both ways. As you extend grace to your partner, it's crucial to also turn that compassionate gaze inward. In the hustle and bustle of modern life, where the roles of partner, parent, and professional often collide, it's all too easy to become your own harshest critic. Practicing self-compassion, not only enhances your own emotional well-being but also enriches your relationships by presenting a healthier, more empathetic version of yourself.

To truly embrace compassion, it needs to be more than just an occasional effort—it should be a consistent practice. Make it a point to check in with each other regularly, using monthly reviews as a way to keep your relationships on track. Reflect on how you've embodied compassion throughout the month and identify areas where you can improve. By doing so, you keep the principle of compassion alive and actionable, making it the foundation of your relationship and family life. Committing to consistent compassion goes beyond simply avoiding conflicts or smoothing over rough patches; it elevates the entire relationship, creating a sanctuary of understanding, respect, and unconditional love. This becomes the model of a healthy relationship that you can pass on to your children, setting them up for a lifetime of compassionate interactions.

As we approach the final chapter of this book, let's take a moment to reflect on the incredible journey we've embarked on together. From the wisdom of ancient civilisations to the complexities of modern relationships, we've delved into the multifaceted dimensions of love, partnership, and personal growth.

Our world is both astonishingly connected and bewilderingly fragmented. The pressures of work, social expectations, and the ceaseless demands of modern life often divert our attention from what truly matters: our relationships. Yet, it is within these relationships, particularly the one with your partner, that we find our greatest joys, deepest meanings, and most profound growth.

Reflection and intention, rituals and practices, growth and consciousness—these are not mere buzzwords but the fundamental building blocks of an extraordinary relationship. They are the tools that empower you to craft your own beautiful fulfilling relationship one that endures and enriches every aspect of your life. And remember, this story doesn't just impact you and your partner; it sets the stage for future generations. Your children, present or future, will look to your relationship as their first and most impactful example of what love should be.

So, what lies ahead in the next chapter of your relationship? It begins today, right now, with the choices you make and the actions you take. Whether it's adopting a new ritual, dedicating time for a monthly relationship review, or simply pausing to express gratitude and love, each small act contributes to the overall health of your relationship. With each choice you're not just creating a relationship; you're crafting a legacy. Together, you stand at the threshold of infinite possibilities. Embrace a commitment to make the most of this incredible journey, armed with timeless wisdom and the tools for modern life.

Take the bold step into this new chapter with confidence. Your future selves will be grateful, your children will learn from you, and the world will be enriched by the love you share. It has been an honour and privilege to share these teachings with you and wish you and your loved ones every happiness.

If this book deeply resonated with you and you're eager to cultivate more love and happiness in your life, I invite you to explore my website at www.nicholefarrow.com. You can also connect with me on social media or download the My Kin app. Discover the Balanced Relationship Blueprint Course, where you'll find practical steps and rituals to create the meaningful relationships and fulfilling family life you and your loved ones truly deserve. Join a vibrant community of like-minded individuals who are dedicated to nurturing their relationships, parenting, and making a positive impact in their communities.

With love and light,
Nichole

Printed in Great Britain
by Amazon